Mel Bay's

Songs of the Jewish People

D1003787

By Jerry Silverman

Visit us on the Web at http://www.melbay.com — E-mail us at email@melbay.com

Contents

LOVE, COURTSHIP, AND MARRIAGE

Vuszhe Vils Tu? . . . . What Do You Want? 6

A Libe, A Libe . . . . A Love, Yes, A Love 8

Tum Balalaika. Play Balalaika 10

Papir Iz Doch Vays . . . . Oh, Paper Is White 12

Libster Mayner . . . . Oh, My Darling 14

Yomi, Yomi 16

Her Nor, Du Sheyn Meyedele . . . . Listen, My Sweet Pretty Girl 18

Gey Ich Mir Shpatsirn . . . . I Go Out A-Strolling 20

Du Meydele, Du Fayns . . . . You Pretty Little Girl 22

Lomir Zich Iberbetn . . . . Let's Make Up 24

Oy, Dortn, Dortn . . . . Away Out Yonder 26

Shvartse Karshelech . . . . Black Cherries 28

CHILDREN AND GRANDCHILDREN

Oyfn Pripetshok . . . . On The Hearth 30

Vigndig A Fremd Kind . . . . Rocking Someone Else's Child 32

Rozhinkes Mit Mandlen . . . . Raisins And Almonds 34

O, Ir Kleyne Lichtelech . . . . Oh, You Little Candle Lights 36

Hulyet, Hulyet, Kinderlech . . . . My Dearest Little Ones 38

A Fidler . . . . A Fiddler 40

LECHAYIM! — TO LIFE!

Lechayim! . . . . To Life! 42

Ale Mentshen Tanstendik . . . . Folks Are At Their Dancingest 43

In Der Kuznye . . . . In The Smithy 44

Di Mechutonim Geyen . . . . The In-Laws Are Arriving 46

Shprayz Ich Mir . . . . Walking Down The Highway 48

Bayt Zhe Mir Oys A Finfuntsvantsiker . . . . . Change For Me This Twenty-Fiver 50

Chatskele, Chatskele 52

Hey! Zhankoye 54

Hamentashn 56

Vi Azoy Trinkt A Keyser Tey? . . . . How Does A Tsar Drink Tea? 58

Achtsik Er Un Zibetsik Zi . . . . Eighty He And Seventy She 60

Di Mezinke Oysgegebn . . . . My Youngest Daughter's Married 62

Ch' bin A Bocher, A Hultay . . . . I'm A Wandering Fellow 64

Kum Aher, Du Filozof . . . . Come To Me, Philosopher 66

Di Ban . . . . The Train 68

Sha! Shtil! . . . . Be Still! 70

Der Rebbe Elimelech . . . . Rabbi Elimelech 72

TEARS OF SORROW — TEARS OF JOY

Dem Milners Trern	The Miller's Tears	76
Yoshke Fort Avek	Yoshke's Leaving Now	78
Mit A Nodl, On A Nodl	With A Needle, Or Without One	80
Shlof, Mayn Kind, Shlof Keseyder	Sleep, My Child, Sleep Securely	82
Ot Azoy Neyt A Shnayder	Stitch Away, Little Taylor	84
Un Du Akerst	Oh, You Plow	86
Dire Gelt	Rent Money	88
Bulbes	Potatoes	90

THE GOLDEN LAND — AMERICA

Elis Ayland	Ellis Island	92
A Briv Fun Amerike	A Letter From America	94
Eyn Zach Vel Ich	Only One Thing I Ask	96
Kolumbus, Ich Hob Tsu Dir Gornit	Columbus, I Give You The First Prize	98
Di Grine Kuzine	The Greenhorn Cousin	100
Eyder Ich Leyg Mich Shlofn	No Sooner Do I Lie Down	102
Mayn Rue Plats	My Resting Place	104
In Kamf	In Struggle	106
To Gey Zich Lernen Tantsn	Just Go And Learn To Dance Now	108

THE HOLOCAUST

Unter Di Churves Fun Poyln	Under The Ruins Of Poland	110
Aroys Iz In Vilne A Nayer Bafel	In Vilna Was Issued A Brand-New Decree	112
Shtil, Di Nacht	Still, The Night	114
Zog Nit Keynmol	Never Say	116

Courtesy N.Y. Public Library Picture Collection

Introduction

Albert Einstein once said, "The Yiddish folk songs, why they are the most sincere, the most heartfelt I have heard anywhere. They are the truest expression of the soul of a people."

One need but glance at the table of contents of this book to see what prompted Einstein's comment. The songs cover the entire gamut of human emotion and experience (and even beyond human experience). They range from the fiddle songs of courtship to rocking the cradle, and from a fiftieth wedding anniversary (set against the backdrop of never-ending labor, poverty, and discrimination in nineteenth-century Eastern Europe) to the new struggles for survival in America and the unbelievable darkness of the Holocaust.

Amazingly, through all this litany of hardship, many of these songs are rich in humor: laughing to keep from crying or just plain laughing (any Jew can sing better than the cantor -- only at the moment he happens to have a cold).

The unifying factor in this great song literature is the language itself: Yiddish. Yiddish is (was) the language of the Jewish people of Eastern and Central Europe. Allowing for regional differences in pronunciation of some vowels and borrowings from local languages, a Jew from the Crimea can converse with a Jew from Amsterdam; a Jew from Vienna can hold forth with a Jew from Paris. It is this universality of the language that has facilitated the survival of so many of these songs despite the ravages of the Holocaust.

American Jews, two or three generations away from their European roots, may find Yiddish slipping away: only recalled in a few expressions or the half-remembered refrain of a song. In recent years this trend has been, to some extent, slowed down (not yet reversed) by the klezmer music revival. Klezmer music is essentially celebratory dance and song (in Yiddish) performed traditionally on joyous occasions such as weddings, bar mitzvahs, and certain holidays.

As noted, the songs in this collection cover a somewhat wider range than those strictly associated with klezmer music. The English translations are singable, but to get "inside" the heart and soul of the material, dust off (if it needs dusting off) your Yiddish and sing them in the original.

Courtesy N.Y. Public Library Picture Collection

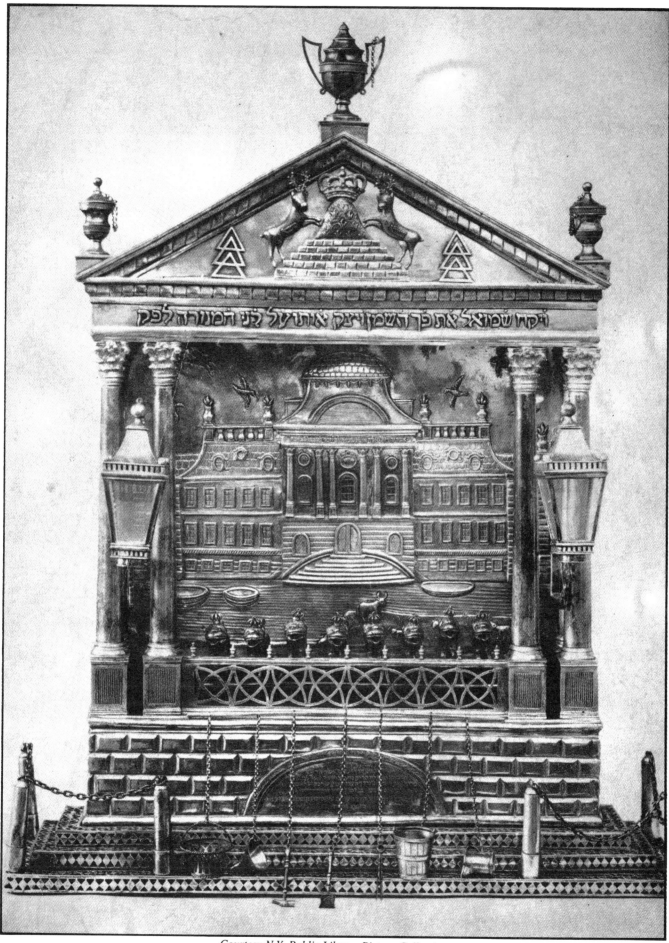

ויקח שמואל את קרן השמן ויצק אותו על לו המורה לפק

Courtesy N.Y. Public Library Picture Collection

5

Vuszhe Vils Tu?
What Do You Want?

Slowly – ad lib

Vus-zhe vils tu, vos-zhe vils tu? A shnay-der far a man? A shnay-der far a man? A
What do you want, what do you want? A tail-or for a man? A tail-or for a man? A

Faster – in tempo

shnay-der far a man vil ich nit! A shnay-ders toch-ter bin ich nit!
tail-or for a man, sure-ly not! A tail-or's daugh-ter I am not!

Kleyd-'lech ney-en ken ich nit! Zits ich oyf-n shteyn, shtil-er-heyt un
Sew-ing dress-es. I can-not! I'll sit on a stone, Qui-et-ly and

veyn. A-le mey-de-lech hob-n cha-se-ne, Nor ich blayb a-leyn.
moan. All the girls, they are get-ting mar-ried, But I am left a-lone.

Vuszhe vils tu, vuszhe vils tu?
A shuster far a man?
A shuster far a man?

    A shuster far a man vil ich nit!
    A shusters tochter bin ich nit!
    Shich lotn ken ich nit!
    Zits ich oyf'n shteyn
    Shtiller hayt un veyn:
    Ale meydelach hobn chasene,
    Nor ich blayb aleyn!

What do you want, what do you want?
A cobbler for a man?
A cobbler for a man?

    A cobbler for a man, surely not!
    A cobbler's daughter, I am not!
    Patching shoes, I cannot!
    I'll sit on a stone
    And I'll weep and moan:
    And the girls, they are getting married,
    But I am left alone.

Vuszhe vils tu, vuszhe vils tu?
A rebbn far a man?
A rebbn far a man?

    A rebbn far a man vil ich doch!
    A rebbns tochter bin ich doch!
    Toyre lernen ken ich doch!
    Zits ich oyf dach
    Un kuk arup un lach:
    Ale meydelach hobn chasene,
    Ich mit zey baglach!

What do you want, what do you want?
A rabbi for a man?
A rabbi for a man?

    A rabbi for a man – that's for me!
    I'm a rabbi's daughter, don't you see!
    Torah learning – certainly!
    I am flying high,
    Laugh until I cry:
    All the girls are getting married,
    And now so am I!

Courtesy N.Y. Public Library Picture Collection

A Libe, A Libe
A Love, Yes, A Love

Vos shteystu unter mayne fenster,
Azoy vi a zelner far der tir?
Tsu bin ich den di tayreste, di shenste?
Vos hostu zich ayngelibt in mir?] 2

You stand by my window and you never rest.
At my door, you're all I ever see.
Am I your dearest and your prettiest?
Why did you fall so in love with me?] 2

A fayer hot gedarft dos hoyz farbrenen,
Eyder ich hob dich dort gezeyn.
Der tayvl hot mich gedarft tsunemen,
Eyder du host zich ayngelibt in mir!] 2

A fire should have burned that house down,
Before I ever you did see.
The devil should have taken me away,
Before you fell so in love with me.] 2

Vest krugn a shenere un a besere,
Zi vet zayn kluger noch far mir.
A berye vet zi oych zayn, a gresere;
Vuszhe hostu zich ayngelibt in mir?] 2

A prettier and better girl you'll surely find.
She'll be wiser than I could ever be.
More skillfull and with a much finer mind;
Why did you fall so in love with me?] 2

Courtesy N.Y. Public Library Picture Collection

Tum Balalaika
Play Balalaika

A balalaika is a three-string, triangular-shaped Russian folk instrument. It is played somewhat like a mandolin with rapid tremolo melodic and chordal passages.

Moderately

Shteyt a boch - er un ___ er tracht, Tracht un tracht di
There's a young man deep ___ in thought, And he won - ders

gan - tse nacht; Ve - men tsu ne - men, un nit far - she - men,
whom ___ he ought To take as wife, men, for all of his life, To

Ve - men tsu ne - men, un nit far - she - men.
take as his wife, for all of his life.

Chorus
Tum ba - la, tum ba - la, tum ba - la - lai - ka, Tum ba - la, tum ba - la,

tum ba - la - lai - ka. Tum ba la la - lai - ka, { Shpil, ba - la - la - / Play, ba - la -

lai - ka, Tum ba - la - lai - ka, Frey - lich zol zayn.
lai - ka, Tum ba - la - lai - ka, Let there be joy.

Meydl, meydl, ich vil bay dir fregn,	Tell me, maiden, I'd like to know,
Vos ken vaksn, vaksn on regn?	What it is needs no rain to grow?
Vos ken brenen un nit oyfheren?	What's not consumed although it's burning?
Vos ken beynkn, veynen on treren? *Chorus*	What weeps no tears although it's yearning? *Chorus*

Narisher bocher, vos darfst du fregn,	You foolish boy, didn't you know,
A shteyn ken vaksn, vaksn on regn.	A stone does not need rain to grow?
A libe ken brenen un nit oyfheren,	A love's not consumed although it's burning,
A hartz ken beynken, veynen on treren. *Chorus*	A heart weeps no tears although it's yearning. *Chorus*

Courtesy N.Y. Public Library Picture Collection

Papir Iz Doch Vays
Oh, Paper Is White

Nechtn banacht bin ich oyf a chasene geven.
Fil sheyne meydelach hob ich dort gezen.
Fil sheyne meydelach — tsu dir kumt nisht gor —
Ts dayne shvartse eygelach, tsu dayne shvartse hor.

Ach du liber Got, varf mir nisht arop,
Glaych mich nit tsu keyn beymele un nit tsu keyn slop.
Dos beymele az es blit iz doch zeyer sheyn;
Vi helft mir shoyn Got mir dir tsu der chupe tsu geyn.

Last night to a wedding I went without care.
A room full of pretty girls I did see there,
A room full of pretty girls — but none to compare
With your pretty coal-black eyes, and your raven hair.

Oh please, dearest God, do not cast me down.
I'm not like a tree or a stick in the ground.
A tree when it blooms is lovely to see;
With God's help, my darling, my bride you will be.

Courtesy Jerry Silverman Collection

13

Libster Mayner
Oh, My Darling

Words by Abarbanel
Music by Ben Yomen

Moderately

S'iz der step shoyn op-ge-sho — rn, Un shoyn alts tsu
Now the fields have all been har-vest — ed, And the crops have

noyf ge-nu — men. Lib — ster may-ner, kum tsu
all been gath — ered. Oh, my dar — ling, come a-

fo — rn; Ich vel var — tn oyf dayn ku — men, hey!
rid — ing; How I wait_ for your ar — ri — val hey!

1.

2. Last time skip this and go to "Final Ending."

To next verse

Final Ending

hey!_____ Un di hey!_____
hey!_____ And the hey!_____

2.

14

Un di karshn, libster mayner,
Zaynen shvartze vi dayne oygn.
Ongeshotn oyf di beymer,
Un di tsvaygn zich aych boygn, hey!] 2

And the cherries, o, my sweetheart,
Like your eyes, they glisten darkly,
Trees are covered over with them,
And their branches, they bend to you, hey!] 2

Kum tsuforn, libster mayner,
Un genug shoyn undz tsu troymen.
Rayf un tsaytig iz mayn libe
Vi s'iz tsaytig mayne floymen, hey!] 2

Come a-riding, o, my sweetheart,
Put an end to all my dreaming;
For my love is ripe and ready,
Like the plums that are so juicy, hey!] 2

Courtesy N.Y. Public Library Picture Collection

15

Yomi, Yomi

Yomi is the girl's name in this conversation between mother and daughter.

Yo - mi, Yo - mi, zing mir a li - de - le, Vos dos may - de - le
Yo - mi, Yo - mi, sing me a lit - tle song, Tell me what do you

vil? Dos mey - de - le vil a por shi - che - lech hob - n,
want? Does my lit - tle girl want a new pair of shoes? Let's

Darf men geyn dem shus - ter - l zog - n. Neyn, ma - me - nyu, neyn, Du
go and tell the cob - bler the news. No, ma - ma, dear, no. That's

kenst mich nit far - shteyn, Du veyst nit vos ich meyn.
not the way to go, I nev - er told you so.

Yomi, Yomi, zing mir a lidele,
Vos dos meydele vil?
Dos meydele vil a kleydele hobn,
Darf men geyn dem shnayderl zogn. *Chorus*

Yomi, Yomi, sing me a little song,
Tell me what do you want?
Does my little girl want a brand-new dress?
Well, I know the tailor's address. *Chorus*

Yomi, Yomi, zing mir a ledele,
Vos dos meydele vil?
Dos meydele vil a chosendl hobn,
Darf men geyn dem shadchendl zogn.

Yomi, Yomi, sing me a little song,
Tell me, what do you want?
Is it for a husband you're sighing,
To the matchmaker, quick, stop your crying.

Final chorus:
Yo, mamenyu, yo,
Du veyst shoyn vos ich meyn,
Du kenst mich shoyn farshteyn!

Final chorus:
Yes, mama dear, yes,
At last you understand
I really want a man.

Courtesy N.Y. Public Library Picture Collection

17

Her Nor, Du Sheyn Meydele
Listen, My Sweet Pretty Girl

Slowly

Her nor, du sheyn mey-de-le, Her nor, du sheyn mey-de-le,
Lis - ten, my sweet pret-ty girl, Lis - ten, my dear pret-ty girl,

Vos ves-tu ton_____ in a - za vay-ten__ veg?
What will you do_____ in such a far - a-way place?

Vos ves-tu ton_____ in a - za vay-ten__ veg?
What will you do_____ in such a far - a-way place?

Ich vel geyn in a - le ga-sen, Ich vel shray-en, "vesh tsu__ vash-en." A-
I will wan-der through the cit - y, Cry - ing, "Clothes washed, please have__ pit - y." As

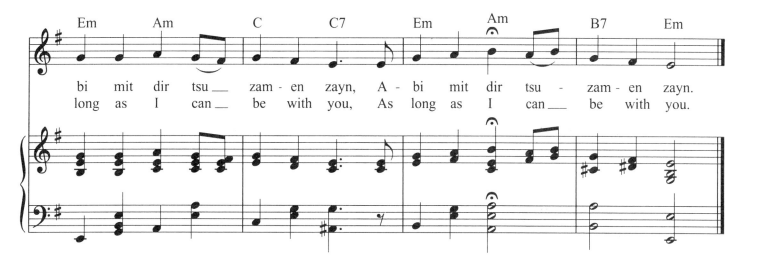

bi mit dir tsu — zam - en zayn, A - bi mit dir tsu - zam - en zayn.
long as I can — be with you, As long as I can — be with you.

1) Her nor, du shayn maydele,
   Her nor, du fayn maydele,
   Vos vestu esn in aza vaytn veg?
   Vos vestu esn in aza vaytn veg?

   Broyt mit zalts vel ich esn,
   Tate-mame vel ich fergesn;
   Abi mit dir tsuzamen zayn,
   Abi mit dir tsuzamen zayn.

2) Her nor, du shayn maydele,
   Her nor, du fayn maydele,
   Oyf vos vestu shlofn in aza vaytn veg?
   Oyf vos vestu shlofn in aza vaytn veg?

   Ich bin noch a yunge froy,
   Ich ken shlofn oyf a bintl shtroy;
   Abi mit dir tsuzamen zayn,
   Abi mit dir tsuzamen zayn.

1) Listen my sweet pretty girl,
   Listen, my dear pretty girl,
   What will you eat in such a faraway place?
   What will you eat in such a faraway place?

   Bread and salt I'll eat with pleasure,
   Parents, I'll forget forever;
   As long as I can be with you,
   As long as I can be with you.

2) Listen, my sweet pretty girl,
   Listen, my dear pretty girl,
   On what will you sleep in such a faraway place?
   On what will you sleep in such a faraway place?

   I'm a young and healthy woman.
   I would sleep on straw with you, man,
   As long as I can be with you,
   As long as I can be with you.

Courtesy N.Y. Public Library Picture Collection

19

Gey Ich Mir Shpatsirn
I Go Out A-Strolling

Gey ich mir shpa - tsi - rn,
I go out a - stroll - ing,
Tra - la - la - la - la - la.

Gey ich mir shpa - tsi - rn,
I go out a - stroll - ing,
Tra - la - la - la - la - la. Ba - I

ge - gnt mich a bo - cher, A - ha! A - ha! Ba -
come a - cross a fel - low, A - ha! A - ha! I

ge - gnt mich a bo - cher, A - ha!
come a - cross a fel - low, A - ha!

Er zogt er vet mich nemen,
    Tra la la la la la. ⎦2

Er leygt es·op oyf vinter,
    Aha! Aha! ⎦2

He told me he would wed me,
    Tra la la la la la. ⎦2

But not before the winter,
    Aha! Aha! ⎦2

Der vinter is gekumen,
    Tra la la la la la. ⎦2

Er hot mich nit genumen,
    Aha! Aha! ⎦2

Well, winter is upon us,
    Tra la la la la la. ⎦2

But he did break his promise,
    Aha! Aha! ⎦2

Itst vil er mich shoyn nemen,
    Tra la la la la la. ⎦2

Ober ich vil im nit kenen,
    Aha! Aha! ⎦2

And now he wants to take me,
    Tra la la la la la. ⎦2

He really does mistake me,
    Aha! Aha! ⎦2

Hasidim, *Lwow*

Courtesy N.Y. Public Library Picture Collection

Du Meydele, Du Fayns
You Pretty Little Girl

Moderately

Du mey-de-le, du fayns, Du mey-de-le, du sheyns, Ich vel dir e - pes
You pret-ty lit-tle girl, You ap-ple of my eye, I have a rid-dle

fre - gn, A re-te-nish, a kleyns: Vos iz hech-er fun ___ a
for ___ you, So an-swer it, please try. What is tall-er than ___ a

hoyz? Un vos iz ___ flin-ker fun ___ a moyz? Du na - ri - sher
house? And what is ___ fast-er than ___ a mouse? You fool-ish young

bo - cher, du na - ri - sher chlop! Host du nit keyn se - chl ___
boy, well, you sure ___ are so dense! Don't you have a bit ___ of ___

22

in ___ dayn ___ kop! Der roych iz hech - er fun _____ a
com - mon ___ sense? For smoke is tall - er than _____ a

hoyz. A kotz iz ___ flin - ker fun _____ a moyz.
house. A cat is ___ fast - er than _____ a mouse.

Du meydele du fayns, du meydele du sheyns,
Ich vel dir epes fregn, a retenish a kleyns:
Vos ken fliyn on a fligl?
Un vos ken moyern on a tsigl?

> Du narisher bocher, du narisher chlop!
> Host doch nit keyn seychl in dayn kop!
> Der shney ken fliyn on a fligl,
> Un der frost ken moyern on a tsigl.

You pretty little girl, you apple of my eye,
I have a riddle for you, so answer it, please try:
What is wingless, but flies quick?
And what can build without a brick?

> You foolish boy, you sure are so dense!
> Don't you have a bit of common sense?
> Snow is wingless, but flies quick.
> Frost can build without a brick.

Du meydele du fayns, du meydele du sheyns,
Ich vel dir epes fregn, a retenish a kleyns:
Vos fara keyser iz on a land?
Un vos fara vaser iz on zamd?

> Du narisher bocher, du narisher chlop!
> Host doch nit keyn seychl in dayn kop!
> Der keyser fun harts hot nit keyn land.
> Trern fun di oygn zenen on zamd.

You pretty little girl, you apple of my eye,
I have a riddle for you, so answer it, please try:
Where is the king who has no land?
And where is the water without sand?

> You foolish boy, you sure are so dense!
> Don't you have a bit of common sense?
> The king of hearts, he has no land.
> The tears that fall, they have no sand.

Lomir Zich Iberbetn
Let's Make Up

1) Lomir zich iberbetn, iberbetn,
   Vos shteystu bay mayn fenster?
   Vos shteystu bay mayn fenster?
   Lomir zich iberbetn,
   Bist bay mir der shenster. ⎤2

2) Lomir zich iberbetn, iberbetn,
   Koyf a por marantsn,
   Koyf a por marantsn.
   Lomir zich iberbetn,
   Lomir geyen tantsn. ⎤2

3) Lomir zich iberbetn, iberbetn,
   Shtel dem samovar,
   Shtel dem samovar,
   Lomir zich iberbetn,
   Zay-zhe nisht kayn nar. ⎤2

4) Lomir zich iberbetn, iberbetn,
   Lomir nisht zayn vi geyrim,
   Lomir nisht zayn vi geyrim.
   Lomir zich iberbetn,
   Lomir zayn chaverim. ⎤2

1) Let's make up once again, let's make up now.
   Please don't stay outside,
   Please don't stay outside.
   Let's make up once again,
   For you're my lovely bride. ⎤2

2) Let's make up once again, let's make up now.
   Oranges we'll buy,
   Oranges we'll buy.
   Let's make up once again,
   Go dancing, you and I. ⎤2

3) Let's make up once again, let's make up now.
   Heat the samovar,*
   Hear the samovar.
   Let's make up once again,
   How silly you now are. ⎤2

4) Let's make up once again, let's make up now.
   We're not like the others,
   We're not like the others.
   Let's make up once again,
   And let us just be lovers. ⎤2

*Samovar —

typical Russian urn used for boiling water for tea.

Courtesy Jerry Silverman Collection

25

Oy, Dortn, Dortn
Away Out Yonder

Oy, dor-tn, dor-tn, i-bern vas-er-l, Oy,
A-way out yon-der, far a-cross the wa-ter, A-

dor-tn, dor-tn, i-ber-n brik,_____ Far-
cross the bridge that leads_ far a-way,_____ They've_

tri-bn hot men mich, in di vay-te-ne len-der, Un
driv-en me a-way into far-off__ coun-tries, And

ben-kn, benk ___ ich noch dir tsu-rik._____
now I long ___ for you ev-'ry day._____

Oy, vifil ovntlech, tsuzamen gezesen,
Oy, vifil ovntlech, shpet in di nacht.
Oy, vifil trerelech mir hobn fargosn,
Oy, biz mir hobn di libe tsuzamen gebracht.

Oy, dayne oygelech, vi di shvartse karshelech,
Un dayne lipelech, vi rozeve papir.
In dayne fingerlech, nem tint un feder,
Oy, shraybn zolstu ofte briv tsu mir.

How many evenings we sat together,
How many evenings, late into the night.
How many were the tears we shed between us.
Until our love set everything aright.

Oh, your sweet little eyes, like the blackest cherries,
And your sweet lips, the color of a rose,
And your sweet fingertips, I hope that you will use them
To write me letters often, goodness knows.

Courtesy N.Y. Public Library Picture Collection

Shvartse Karshelech
Black Cherries

Lively waltz

Shvar - tse kar - she - lech rayst men,_____ Un gri - ne
Ripe black cher - ries are gath - ered,_____ The green ne are

lozt_____ men shteyn;_____ Shey - ne mey - de - lech
left on the tree;_____ Pret - ty girls do get

nemt men,_____ Un mi - se lozt_____ men geyn._____
cho - sen,_____ For - got - ten are the ug - ly._____

Chorus

Oy, vey iz tsu mir._____ Un vey tsu
Oh, woe un - to me, _____ I have shed

Vos toyg mir di polke-mazurke,
Az tantsn tants ich zi nit.
Vos toyg mir dos meydele fun Vurke,
Az libn libt zi mich nit. *Chorus*

Vos toyg mir der nayer valets –
Az tantsn tants ich im nisht.
Vos toyg mir dos meydele fun Shilets,
Az libn libt zi mich nisht. *Chorus*

Vos toygn mir di lipelech, di sheyne,
Az kushn, kushn zey mich nit?
Vos toygn mir di hentelech, di kleyne,
Az gletn, gletn zey mich nit? *Chorus*

What good is the polka-mazurka?
My heart is not carefree.
What good is the maiden from Vurka,
When she does not love me? *Chorus*

The brand-new waltzes don't thrill me –
Let others go to the ball.
The girl from Shilets, she'll kill me,
For she doesn't love me at all. *Chorus*

What good do her lips do me?
For I never get a kiss.
Her little hands don't come to me,
I never get a caress. *Chorus*

Oyfn Pripetshok
On The Hearth

Mark Warshawsky (1848-1907) has been called the Yiddish Robert Burns. Comparing him also to Woody Guthrie would not be far from the truth either. In his lifetime, as also happened with the Scottish bard and the Okie balladeer, the songs of Mark Warshawsky came to be regarded as genuine folk songs. He practiced law in Kiev–not too successfully–while composing for his own pleasure, and the pleasure of his friends, songs mirroring Russian-Jewish life as he knew it. However, it was not until 1899 that he began to achieve widespread recognition for his works. In that year the writer Sholem Aleichem first heard Warshawsky's songs. He immediately recognized their true worth and a fast friendship grew between the two men. They frequently performed together, Sholem Aleichem reading from his works and Warshawsky singing his. In 1900 a first edition of his *Yidishe Folkslider (Yiddish Folk Songs),* published in Kiev, sold out. Warshawsky dreamed of going to America and performing his material there, but he never did. In 1918, Sholem Aleichem brought out the second edition of *Yidishe Folkslider* in New York.

By Mark Warshawsky

Moderately

Oy - fn pri - pe - tshok brent a fa - ye - rl, Un in shtub iz heys;
Oh, the fi - re burns in the glow-ing hearth, And the room is hot;

Un - der reb - be le - rent kley-ne kin - der lech dem__ a - lef - beys;
And the rab - bi teach-es all the lit - tle boys The__ al - pha - bet;

Un - der reb - be le - rent kley-ne kin - der lech dem__ a - lef - beys.
And the rab - bi teach-es all the lit - tle boys the__ al - pha - bet.

30

Lernt kinder, mit groys cheyshek,
Azoy zog ich on;
Ver s'vet gicher fun aych kenen "Ivre," ⌉ 2
Der bakumt a fon. ⌋ *Chorus*

Learn your lessons well, with great interest,
That is what I say.
He who gets to know his Hebrew best of all ⌉ 2
Wins a prize today. ⌋ *Chorus*

Lernt kinder, hot nit moyre,
Yeder onhoyb iz shver;
Gliklech iz der vos lernt Toyre, ⌉ 2
Tsi darf der mentsh noch mer? ⌋ *Chorus*

Learn your lessons well, do not be afraid,
Hardest is the start.
Happy is the man who learns the Torah well, ⌉ 2
Clasps it to his heart. ⌋ *Chorus*

Ir vet, kinder, elter vern,
Vet ir aleyn farshteyn,
Vifil in di oysyes lign trern, ⌉ 2
Un vifil geveyn. ⌋ *Chorus*

Children, you will learn, when you're older,
You'll know all too well,
Of the tears that lie in every letter – ⌉ 2
More than tongue can tell. ⌋ *Chorus*

Az ir vet, kinder dem goles shlepn,
Oysgemutshet zayn,
Zolt ir fun di oysyes koyech shepn, ⌉ 2
Kukt zey arayn! ⌋ *Chorus*

If it happens that you should be exiled,
Suffering great pain,
From these letters may you gain your strength; ⌉ 2
Look at them again. ⌋ *Chorus*

Vigndig A Fremd Kind
Rocking Someone Else's Child

(The Baby-Sitter's Complaint)

Zolst a-zoy le-bn, Un zayn ge-zint, Vi ich vel dir zi-tsn Un
You can't im-ag-ine, It drives me wild, To sit here all day And to

vi-gn s'kind. Ay-lyu-lyu, Sha-sha-sha! Dayn
rock this child. Hush-a-bye, Don't you cry! Your

ma-me-shi z'ge-gan-gen In mark a-rayn. Ay-lyu-lyu,
ma-ma, she has gone out, Some food to buy. Hush-a-bye,

Shlof, mayn kind; Di ma-me-shi vel-ku-men Gich un g'shvind.
Sleep, my child; your ma-ma will re-turn In just a while.

Zolst azoy lebn,	I can't take it,
S'geyt mir derinen!	It's just not fair –
Dayn mameshi z'gegangen	Your mother has gone off
In mark arayn fardinen. *Chorus*	To work somewhere. *Chorus*
Andere meydelech	Other young girls
Tantsen un shpringen,	Dance and play,
Un ich muzn' kind	While here by the cradle
Vign un zingen! *Chorus*	I must stay. *Chorus*
Andere meydelech	Other young girls
Tsukerkelech nashn,	Candies are *noshing,* *
Un izh muzn's kind,	And I've got a pile of
Vindelech vashn! *Chorus*	Diapers for washing. *Chorus*

Noshing (yiddish-English) - snacking, nibbling

Courtesy N.Y. Public Library Picture Collection

33

Rozhinkes Mit Mandlen
Raisins And Almonds

By Abraham Goldfaden

O, Ir Kleyne Lichtelech
Oh, You Little Candle Lights

A Song for Chanuka

By Morris Rosenfeld

Moderately

O, ir kley - ne lich - te - lech, Ir der - tseylt __ ge -
Oh, you lit - tle can - dle - lights, Burn - ing for __ eight

shich - te - lech, May - se - lech on __ a tsol. ___
days and nights, Won - der - ful tales __ you tell. ___

Ir der - tseylt fun blu - ti - keyt. Ber - ye - shaft un mu - ti -
Bat - tles fought 'gainst sla - ver - y. Skill and blood and brav - er -

keyt. Vun - der fun a - mol. ___ fun a - mol. ___
y. Long a - go be - fell. ___ go be - fell. ___

Ven ich ze aych finklendik,	When your twinkling lights I see,
Kumt a cholem pintlendik,	Then a dream appears to me,
Ret an alter troym.	Dream of long ago.
Yid, du host gekrigt amol,	Jew, in battles you did stand,
Yid, du host gekrigt amol, ⎤ 2	Jew, with vict'ries in your hand, ⎤ 2
Ach, dos gloybt zich koym. ⎦	Where did those times go? ⎦

Courtesy N.Y. Public Library Picture Collection

Hulyet, Hulyet, Kinderlech
Play, My Dearest Little Ones

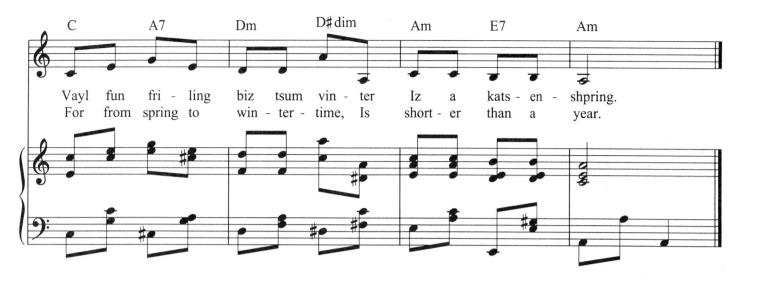

Shpilt aych, libe kinderlech,	Play, my dearest little ones,
Farzoymt keyn oygenblik,	And do not waste your time,
Farzoymt keyn oygenblik.	And do not waste your time.
Nemt mich oych arayn in shpil, ⎤ 2	Let me join you in your game – ⎤ 2
Fargint mir oych dos glik? ⎦ *Chorus*	Can all your joy be mine? ⎦ *Chorus*

Kukt nisht oyf mayn groyen kop,	Don't look at my graying head,
Tsi shtert dos aych in shpil?	Does it disturb your fun?
Tsi shtert dos aych in shpil?	Does it disturb your fun?
Mayn neshome iz noch yung, ⎤ 2	For my soul is still as young ⎤ 2
Vi ts'rik mit yorn fil. ⎦ *Chorus*	As 'twas in years bygone. ⎦ *Chorus*

Mayn neshome iz noch yung,	Yes, my soul, it is still young,
Un geyt fun benkshaft oys,	And longingly does pine,
Un geyt fun benkshaft oys.	And longingly does pine.
Ach, vi gern vilt zich ir ⎤ 2	Oh, how gladly would it rise up, ⎤ 2
Fun altn guf aroys. ⎦ *Chorus*	And go back in time. ⎦ *Chorus*

Shpilt aych, libe kinderlech,	Play, my dearest little ones,
Farzoymt keyn oygenblik,	And do not waste your time,
Farzoymt keyn oygenblik.	And do not waste your time.
Vayl der friling ekt zich bald, ⎤ 2	For the springtime will soon end – ⎤ 2
Mit im dos hechste glik. ⎦ *Chorus*	With it your joy sublime. ⎦ *Chorus*

A Fidler
A Fiddler

Moderately

S'hot der ta-te fun ya-rid-l - Mir ge-bracht a na-ye fi-dl.
Once, when I was ve-ry lit-tle, Pa-pa brought me home a fid-dle.

Do re mi fa sol la si,
{ Shpil ich di-dl, di, di._____
{ I play did-dle, dee, dee._____

Shpil ich di-dl, di, di.
I play did-dle dee, dee.

Ch'halt dos kepl ongeboygen,	Hold my head at the right angle,
Un farglots di beyde oygn. *Chorus*	Do not let the fiddle dangle. *Chorus*
Rechtn fus faroys a bisl,	With my right foot out I must stand,
Klap dem takt tsu mitn fisl. *Chorus*	Counting, tapping, "One and, two-and." *Chorus*
Kvelt un vundert zich di mame,	Mama can't keep herself steady,
"Kenst doch azoy gut di game!" *Chorus*	"See, he knows the scale already!" *Chorus*

Courtesy Jerry Silverman Collection

Lechayim!
To Life!

Lively

Le - cha - yim, Yi - de - lech! Le - cha - yim, bri - der - lech!
To life, my fel - low Jews! To life, my broth - er Jews!

Zingt zhe, trinkt zhe, A - le in a gu - ter sho!
Sing now, drink now, That is what good times are for!

To, lo - mir hul - ye - nen, A - rayn zich kul - ye - nen
Let's keep on swag - ger - ing. And we'll be stag - ger - ing

In dem gan - ey - dn Bol - she ni - tshe - vo!
To Pa - ra - dise, And there is noth - ing more!

Ale Mentshen Tantzendik
Folks Are At Their Dancingest

Each verse begins with a repeat of the first eleven measures of text and music.

...Es iz shoyn tsayt esn geyn!   ...It's time to start feasting, oh, my!

...Es iz shoyn tsayt a mitsve tentsl geyn!   ...It's time to dance with the couple, oh, my!

...Es iz shoyn tsayt shlofn tsu geyn!   ...It's time that we were all sleeping, oh, my!

Chupe – The wedding canopy

In Der Kuznye
In The Smithy

By Shmuel Aychel

In der kuz-nye bay dem fay - er, Shteyt der shmi- der, un er
In the smith-y, by the fi - re, Stands the black- smith, tall and

shmidt. Er klapt dos ay - zn, fun- ken fay- er fli - en,
strong. He strikes the an - vil, sparks of fi - re scat - ter,

Un er zingt der- bay a lid.___ Er klapt dos lid.
And he sings a lust- y song.___ He strikes the song.

Fun der frayhayt vos vet kumen,
Zingt er mutik, zingt er heys;
Un er shpirt nit vi es gist zich
Fun zayn ponim taychn shveys.] 2

Sings of freedom that is coming,
And his brave song rocks the place.
But he takes no notice of the streams
Of perspiration on his face,] 2

Shtark batsoybert fun der frayhayt,
Zingt er vayter un es klingt,
Nor der hamer klapt noch hecher
Un er hert nit vos er zingt.] 2

Thoughts of freedom are enchanting;
He keeps singing, and it rings.
But the hammer, it beats stronger,
And he hears not what he sings.] 2

Fun der erd batsirt mit blumen
Zingt er vayter in zayn lid;
Opgekilt iz shoyn dos ayzn
Un er klapt un vert nit mid.] 2

Of the earth bedecked with flowers,
He continues on, inspired.
Now his anvil's growing cooler,
Still he strikes and is not tired.] 2

Courtesy N.Y. Public Library Picture Collection

Di Mechutonim Geyen
The In-Laws Are Arriving

By Mark Warshawsky

Di me-chu-to-nim gey-en, kin - der, Lo-mir zich frey-en, Shat nor, shat! Der
Now all the in-laws are ar - riv - ing, Let's all be hap-py, Come and see! The

cho-sn iz gor a vun - der, Shpilt a li-de-le dem cho-sns tsad.
bride-groom is just a won - der, Play a song just for his fam-i-ly

Chorus

Ay - ay, ay - ay - ay, ay - ay, ay___ ay,___ ay!

Ay - ay - ay, ay-ay - ay, ay-ay-ay-ay, ay - ay - ay.

Dem chosns shvester Freydl,
Zi dreyt zich vi a dreydl – shat nor, shat!
Nemt zi arayn redl
Un shpilt a lidele dem chosns tsad. *Chorus*

The bridegroom's sister, Freydl,
Like a top spins – come and see!
Take her into the circle
And play a song for his family. *Chorus*

Ot geyt der feter Mindik,
Vos hobn mir gezindikt – shat nor, shat!
Er blozt zich vi an indik,
Shplit a lidele dem chosns tsad. *Chorus*

Now, here comes Uncle Mindik,
Have we ever wronged him? – come and see!
He's puffed up like a turkey;
Play a song just for his family. *Chorus*

Dort geyt Elye dem chosns feter,
Dem baychl glet er – shat nor, shat!
Er iz feter fun ale feters,
Shpilt a lidele dem chosns tsad. *Chorus*

Here come Elye, the bridegroom's uncle,
He pats his belly – come and see!
He's fatter than all others;
Play a song just for his family. *Chorus*

Courtesy N.Y. Public Library Picture Collection

Shprayz Ich Mir
Walking Down The Highway

Lively

Words by S. Kahn

Music by
E. Teitelbaum

System 1 (Am / E7 / Am Dm Am / B7)

Shprayz ich mir mit gi-che mit__ gi - che trit.
Walk-ing down the high-way, I__ set my course.

System 2 (Em / B7 / Em Am Em / E7)

Noch a fer-dl tsum ya-rid,__ tsum ya - rid.
Go-ing to the mar-ket to__ buy a horse.

System 3 (Am / Dm / Am E7 A A7)

Mit-n tay-ster kling ich mir,__ kling ich mir,
With my purse a jing-ling to__ give ich good cheer,_____

System 4 (Dm / E7 / Am D Am)

Un a li-dl zing ich mir,__ zing ich mir.
And a song I'm sing-ing, I'm__ sing - ing clear.

48

Tsu der shtot iz vayt noch, zeyer vayt,
Shteyt a kretshme bay der zayt, bay der zayt,
Breyt tseefnt iz di tir, iz di tir.
Kretshmer, gib a glezl, a glezl mir!

Noch a glezl, noch eyns, noch a gloz
Gist mir on der bale – der balebos.
Vos mir shtot un ven mir, ven yarid,
Az keyn ferdl darf ich nit, darf ich nit.

S'ferdl hob ich nit gekoyft, nit gekoyft,
Un dos gelt shoyn lang farzoyft, lang farzoyft,
Un far tsores shpring ich mir, shpring ich mir,
Un a lidl zing ich mir, zing ich mir,

But the town is far off, it's far away.
I come to a tavern along the way.
And the door is open, it's open wide,
So to wet my whistle I step inside.

I'll just have another and then one more.
Willingly a glassfull the boss does pour.
Where was I just going with all this speed –
To buy a horse? That's something I do not need.

I didn't buy the horse, that's all I can say.
And my money long since is drunk away.
And my troubles make me keep springing on,
And a song I'm singing – I'm singing on.

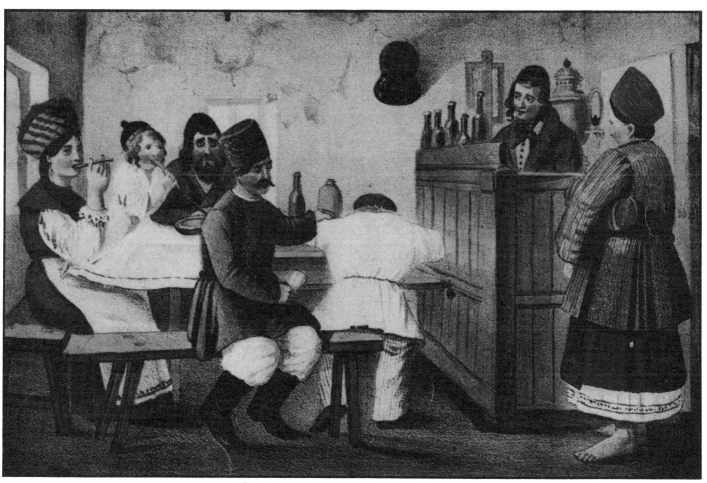

Courtesy N.Y. Public Library Picture Collection

Bayt Zhe Mir Oys A Finfuntsvantsiker
Change For Me This Twenty-Fiver

Freely

Bayt zhe mir oys a finf-un-tsvan-tsi-ker, Oyf sa-me-rod-ne dray-er; Un shpilt zhe mir, klez-mo-rim-lech, A li-de-le, a tay-er.

Change for me, please, this twen-ty-five-er,* In-to a brand-new "three-er;" And play for me, mu-si-cians, play, A song that I hold dear-er.

a tempo

Yam-tshe ram-tshi, yam-tshe ram-tshi, Yam-tshe ram-tshi, yam-tshe-ray; Yam-tshe-ray!

*Ruble note, that is.

50

Bayt zhe mir oys a finfuntsvantsiker
Oyf samerodne firer;
Un shpilt zhe mir, klezmorimlech,
Dos zelbike, vos frier. *Chorus*

Change for me, please, this twenty-fiver
Into a brand-new four,
And play for me, musicians, play,
The one you played before. *Chorus*

Bayt zhe mir oys a finfuntsvantsiker,
Oyf samerodne tsener;
Un shpilt zhe mir, klezmorimlech,
Dos zelbike, nor shener. *Chorus*

Change for me, please, this twenty-fiver
Into a brand-new ten,
And play for me, musicians, play,
The same song once again. *Chorus*

Bayt zhe mir oys a finfuntsvantsiker
Oyf same imperyaln;
Ich vel betn di klezmorimlech,
Zey zoln zich nit ayln. *Chorus*

Change for me, please, this twenty-fiver,
This gold coin's theirs, don't worry;
And I will ask all the musicians, please,
To play but not to hurry. *Chorus*

Courtesy N.Y. Public Library Picture Collection

Chatskele, Chatskele

*Kazatskele -- diminutive of kazatske, a fast Cossack dance.

Nit kayn gebetene, aleyn gekumen,
Chotsh an orime, fort a mume. *Chorus.*

We're uninvited, we came anyway,
Even though she's poor, Auntie, please let her stay. *Chorus.*

Chatskele, chatskele, shpil mir a dume,
Chotsh an orime, abi a frume. *Chorus.*

Chatskele, Chatskele, come on now and play for me.
Even though we're poor, still pious Jews are we. *Chorus.*

Di Kleyne Klezmorim
Courtesy Jerry Silverman Collection

Hey! Zhankoye

Zhankoye was a Jewish settlement in the Crimea in the 1930s. It was completely destroyed by the Germans during World War II.

Enfert Yidn oyf mayn kashe:
Vi'z mayn brider, vi'z Abrashe?
S'geyt bay im der traktor vi a ban.
Di mime Leye ba der kosilke,
Beyle bay der molotilke,
In Zhankoye, zhan, zhan, zhan.   *Chorus*

Ver zogt az Yidn kenen nor handlen,
Essen fette yoich mit mandlen
Nor nit zayn kayn arbetsman?
Dos kenen zogen nor di sonim
Yidn, shpayt zey on in ponim!
Tut a kuk oyf zhan, zhan, zhan.   *Chorus*

If you ask a Jewish farmer,
Where's my brother, where's Abram?
He's driving on his tractor like a train.
The women operate machines,
It's all beyond your wildest dreams,
In Zhankoye, zhan, zhan, zhan.   *Chorus*

Who says that Jews know business only
We've all heard that old baloney
And not be a working man?
Our enemies are in disgrace,
Jews will spit right in their faces,
Take a look at zhan, zhan, zhan.   *Chorus*

Hamentashn

Hamentashn are traditional, triangle-shaped pastries filled with sweet fruit confections. They are baked (and eaten!) during the spring holiday of Purim to commemorate the overthrow of the Persian tyrant, Haman, as recounted in the Book of Esther.

Yach - ne Dvo - she fort in shtot, Zi halt zich in eyn - pak - n,
Yach - ne Dvo - she's going to town, She is - n't fin - ished pack - ing,

Far oyf Pu - rim koyf - n mel,___ Ham - en - tash - en bak - n.
Wants to bake___ some ham - en tash - en, Flo - ur she is lack - ing.

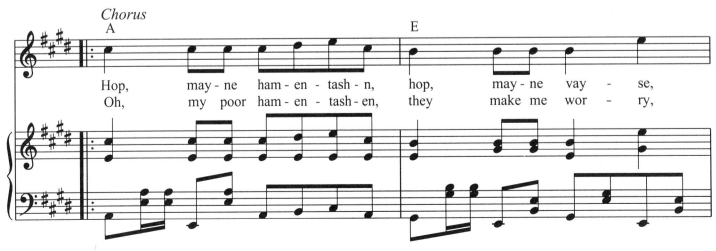

Chorus

Hop, may - ne ham - en - tash - n, hop, may - ne vay - se,
Oh, my poor ham - en - tash - en, they make me wor - ry,

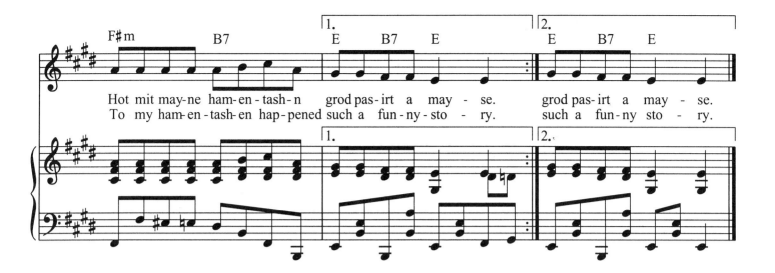

Hot mit may-ne ham-en-tash-n grod pas-irt a may-se. grod pas-irt a may-se.
To my ham-en-tash-en hap-pened such a fun-ny-sto-ry. such a fun-ny sto-ry.

S'geyt a regn, s'geyt a shney
Es kapet fun di decher.
Yachne fort shoyn koyfn mel
In a zak mit lecher. *Chorus*

Nisht kayn honig, nisht kayn mon,
Un fargessen heyvn,
Yachne macht shoyn hamentashn,
Es bakt zich shoyn in oyvn. *Chorus*

Yachne trogt shoyn shalachmones,
Tsu der bobe Yente,
Tsvey, dray hamentashn
Halb-roy, halb-farbrente. *Chorus*

Rain is falling, so is snow,
Every where it's dripping.
Yachne's off to get her flour,
But her sack is ripping. *Chorus*

She's forgotten poppy seeds,
She's forgotten honey,
She's forgotten leavening –
This is getting funny. *Chorus*

Now she's offering them around,
Her pace hasn't slackened.
Two or three poor hamentashen,
Half-raw and half-blackened. *Chorus*

Vi Azoy Trinkt A Keyser Tey?
How Does A Tsar Drink Tea?

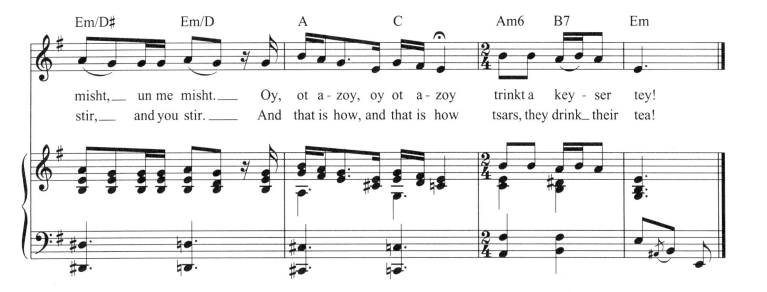

misht,___ un me misht.___ Oy, ot a-zoy, oy ot a-zoy trinkt a key-ser tey!

stir,___ and you stir. ____ And that is how, and that is how tsars, they drink_ their tea!

Each verse begins with a repeat of the first ten measures of text and music.

Vi est a keyser bulbes?
Me shtelt avek a vant mit puter,
Un a soldatl mit a harmatl
Shist durch di puter mit a heyser bulbe,
Un treft dem keyser glaych in moyl arayn.
Oy, ot azoy, oy ot azoy
Est a keyser bulbes.

How does a tsar eat potatoes?
You raise up a big wall of butter,
And a soldier with a cannon
Shoots a hot potato through the butter,
And hits the tsar right in the mouth.
And that's how, and that's how
Tsars eat potatoes.

Vi shluft a keyser bay nacht?
Me shitt un a fuln cheyder mit feydern,
Un me shlaydert arayn ahintsu dem keyser,
Un dray rotes soldatn shteyen un shrayen:
"Sha! Sha! SHA!"
Oy, ot azoy, oy, ot azoy,
Shluft a keyser bay nacht!

How does a tsar sleep at night?
You fill up a room with feathers,
And you throw the tsar into it.
And three companies of soldiers stand and shout,
"Sha! Sha! SHA!"
And that's how, and that's how
Tsars, they sleep at night.

Courtesy N.Y. Public Library Picture Collection

Achtsik Er Un Zibetsik Zi
Eighty He And Seventy She

Es iz hay - nt a - ku - rat ge - vo - ren fuf - tsik yor, Az zey
Well, to - day we mark the fif - tieth an - ni - ver - sa - ry, The old

le - bn shoyn in ey - nem dos al - te por. Zey ho - bn zich ge - el - tert
cou - ple is to - geth - er so hap - pi - ly. They both have got - ten old - er

kikt aych tsi: Ach - tsik er un zi - be - tsik zi.
just you see: Eight - y he and sev - en - ty she.

Chotsh der zeyde mit der bobn zaynen kurts un kleyn,
Nor der zayde mit der bobn zaynen mole cheyn.
Er mitn shpitsichdikn berdele,
Achtsik er un zibetsik zi.

Though the grandpa and the grandma, they are short and small,
Still the grandpa and the grandma are the best of all.
He with his little pointed beard, just you see,
Eighty he and seventy she.

Zey zaynen haynt gegangen beyde in shul,
Un hobn dort gedavnt take ful.
Got hot zey geholfn, borochi,
Achtsik er un zibetsik zi.

Well, today they went together to the *shul,**
And both together they prayed their full.
God has helped them, don't you see?
Eighty he and seventy she.

Der oylem hot zich keyn aynhore gezetst tsum tish,
Un az men hot aroyfgegebn di fayerdike fish,
Hot a droshe gezogt Reb Hershele Tsvi:
Achtsik er un zibitsik zi.

When the guests, thank God, were seated and began to eat,
The spicy fish was served up – what a treat!
A toast was made by Reb Hershele Tsvee:
Eighty he and seventy she.

Shul – prayer house, synagogue

Courtesy N.Y. Public Library Picture Collection

Di Mezinke Oysgegebn
My Youngest Daughter's Married

Motl! Shimen!
Di orime layt zenen gekumen,
Shtelt zey dem shenstn tish,
Tayere vaynen, tayere fish,
Oy vey, tochter, gib mir a kish! *Chorus*

Motl! Shimen!
Here come poor men and women.
Let them have a place to sit,
The wine, the fish – tasty bit.
Kiss me, my child – imagine it! *Chorus*

Ayzik! Mazik!
Di bobe geyt a kazik.
Keyn aynhore zet nor zet,
Vi zi topet, vi zi geyt,
Oy, a simche, oy, a freyd.   *Chorus*

Isaac! Be quick!
See grandma dance a *kazik.* *
Lord protect her, just you see
How she's stamping happily.
What a party – can it be? *Chorus*

Itsik! Shpitsik!
Vos shvaygstu mit dem shmitsik?
Oyf di klezmer tu a geshrey:
Tsi shpiln zey, tsi shlofn zey?
Rayst di strunes ale oyf tsvey!   *Chorus*

Izzy! Dizzy!
Your fiddle should be busy!
To the bandsmen give a shout,
What's this silence all about?
Make those strings sing or get out! *Chorus*

Kazik – a fast, lively Russian dance

Courtesy N.Y. Public Library Picture Collection

Ch'bin A Bocher, A Hultay
I'm A Wandering Fellow

Lively

Ch'bin a bo-cher, a hul-tay, Hob ich mir a shtek - n.
I'm a wan-der-ing fel - low. Some-thing of a rov - er.

Tri - li li - li, tri-li li - li lay Ch'shpan in al di ek - n.
Tri - li li - li, tri-li li - li lay And I've been all o - ver.

Kum ich tsu a kretshme tsu
Klap ich on in toyer.
"Ver biztu? Ver biztu?"
Enfer ich: "A geyer."

I come to a friendly inn,
And I bang the knocker.
"Who are you, say, who are you?"
I reply: "A walker!"

"Leydig-geyer azoy fri,
Chutspenik farshayter!"
Tri-li li-li, tri-li li-li-li,
Un ich gey mir vayter.

"Why so early, please tell us?
Lazy good-for-nothing!"
Tri-li li-li, tri-li li-li-li,
I continue wandering.

Kum ich tsu a brunim tsu
Trink zich on mit vasser,
Shtey ich in dem morgn groy
Vi a hon a nasser.

If I come upon a well,
There my thirst I'm slaking.
Like a wet hen I arise,
When the day is breaking.

Fort a poyerl farbay:
"Tso slichatsh na svetshe?"
Veys ich nit un tu a bray:
"Svetshe, petshe, metshe!"

Comes a peasant riding by:
"What's the latest news?"
How should I know? And I shout,
"Newsy – shmoozey – boozey!"

Courtesy N.Y. Public Library Picture Collection

Kum Aher, Du Filozof
Come To Me, Philosopher

A damf-shif hostu oysgeklert,
Un nemst zich mit dem iber;
Der rebe shpreyt zayn tichl oys
Un shpant dem yam ariber.   *Chorus*

You designed a big steamboat,
It caused a big commotion,
The rabbi spreads his handkerchief
And sails across the ocean.   *Chorus*

A luft-balon hostu oysgetracht
Un meynst du bist a chorets;
Der rebe shpot, der rebe lacht–
Er darf dos oyf kapores.   *Chorus*

You designed an air balloon,
And you brag about it.
The rabbi scoffs – the rabbi laughs,
For he can fly without it.   *Chorus*

Tsu veystu vos der rebe tit
Beshas er zitst bi'ychides–
In eyn minut er in himl flit
Un pravet dort shalesh-sides.   *Chorus*

What does our rabbi do
When we alone do leave him?
Up to the skies he quickly flies–
The heavenly hosts receive him. *Chorus*

Courtesy N.Y. Public Library Picture Collection

Di Ban
The Train

The arrival of the railroad in small towns during the nineteenth century often caused great consternation among the local population. One Kansas farmer rode into town to see the iron horse come through. There he came upon the great, hissing, smoking beast standing in the station. Scratching his head skeptically, he said: "It'll never go." Then, as the train pulled away, gathering speed, he opined: "It'll never stop."

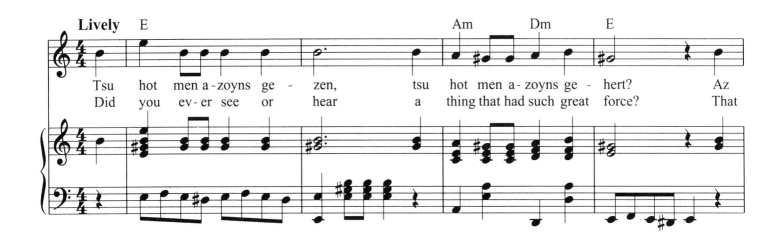

Tsu hot men a-zoyns ge-zen, tsu hot men a-zoyns ge-hert? Az
Did you ev-er see or hear a thing that had such great force? That

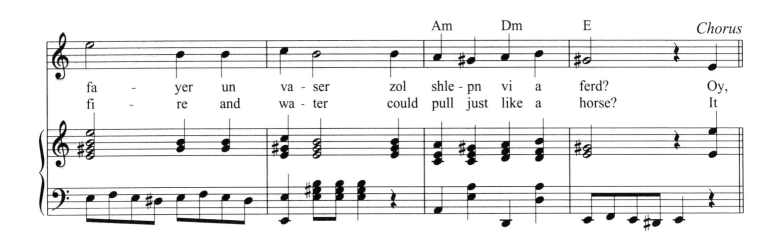

fa - yer un va-ser zol shle-pn vi a ferd? Oy,
fi - re and wa-ter could pull just like a horse? It

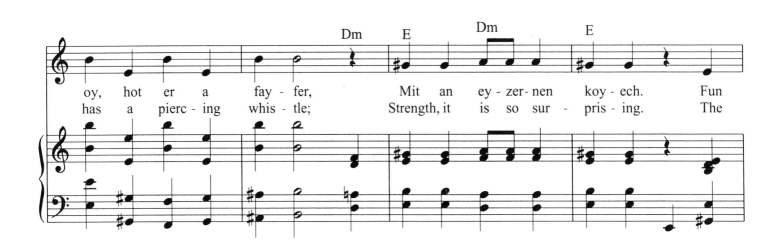

oy, hot er a fay-fer, Mit an ey-zer-nen koy-ech. Fun
has a pierc-ing whis-tle; Strength, it is so sur-pris-ing. The

un - ten gist zich va - ser, Fun oy - ven geyt a roy - ech.
wa - ter pours from un - der A - bove, the steam is ris - ing.

Heyse koyln zenen far im a maychl,
Zudendik vaser zapt er in zayn baychl. *Chorus*

It delights in eating hot coals a-burning,
And the boiling water in its belly churning. *Chorus*

Reboyne-shel-oylem, farkorts im zayne yoren,
Az Yidn apikorsim zoln nit kenen shabes forn. *Chorus*

Oh, dearest Lord God, preserve us from the devil,
And do not let unpious Jews upon the Sabbath travel. *Chorus*

Jewish refugees leaving Russia.
Courtesy N.Y. Public Library Picture Collection

Sha! Shtil!
Be Still!

II Un az der rebe tantst,
   Tantst doch mit der tish,
   Lomir ale topen mit di fis.

I Sha! Shtil! Macht nisht keyn gerider,
  Der rebe geyt shoyn zingn vider.
  Sha! Shtil! Macht nisht keyn gevalt,
  Der rebe geyt shoyn tantsn bald.

II Un az der rebe zingt
   Dem heylign nign,
   Blaybt der sotn a toyter lign.

I Sha! Shtil! Macht nisht keyn gerider,
  Der rebe geyt shoyn zingn vider.
  Sha! Shtil! Macht nisht keyn gevalt,
  Der rebe geyt shoyn zingn bald.

II And when he starts to dance,
   Tables join the beat.
   Let us all start stamping with our feet.

I Be! Still! Talking would be wrong,
  The rabbi wants to sing a song.
  Be! Still! Do not say a thing,
  The rabbi is about to sing.

II And when the rabbi sings
   The holy melody,
   Satan falls for all eternity.

I Be! Still! Talking would be wrong,
  The rabbi wants to sing a song.
  Be! Still! Do not say a thing,
  The rabbi is about to sing.

Courtesy N.Y. Public Library Picture Collection

Der Rebbe Elimelech
Rabbi Elimelech

Slowly – recitative

Az der Re - be E - li - me - lech Iz ge - vo - ren zey - er frey - lach, Iz ge -
E - li - me - lech, o - ur rab - bi, Once was feel - ing ve - ry hap - py; E - li -

vo - ren ze - yer frey - lach, E - li - me - lech, Hot er
me - lech, he was feel - ing ve - ry hap - py. His phy _

oys - ge - ton di tfi - len, Un hot on - ge - ton di bri - len, Un hot ge -
lac - te - ries he took off, And his glass - es near - ly shook off, And then he

Slowly – a tempo　　　　　　　　　　　　　**Gradually faster until the end**

shikt noch di fid - lers, di tsvey. Un az di fi - del - di - ke fid - lers ho - bn
called for his fid - dlers to play. And when the fid - dle - play - ing fid - dlers start - ed

72

Un az der Rebe Elimelech	Elimelech, our rabbi,
Iz gevoren noch mer freylach,	Started feeling still more happy,
Iz gevoren noch mer freylach, Elimelech,	Elimelech started feeling still more happy.
Hot er oysgeton dem hitl,	Then his cap, it went a-twirling,
Un hot ongeton dem kitl,	And his cape, it went a-swirling,
Un hot geshikt noch di tsimblers, di tsvey.	And his tsimbalom players did play.

Un az di tsimbeldike tsimblers	And when the tsimbaloming tsimblers
Hobn tsimbeldik getsimbelt,	Started tsimble-tsimble-tsimbling,
Hobn tsimbeldik getsimbelt, hobn zey,	Started tsimble-tsimble-tsimbling, right away,
Un az di tsimbeldike tsimblers	And when the tsimbaloming tsimblers
Hobn tsimbeldik getsimbelt,	Started tsimble-tsimble-tsimbling,
Hobn tsimbeldik getsimbelt, hobn zey.	How those nimble tsimbalomers, they could play!

Un az der Rebe Elimelech	Elimelech, our rabbi,
Iz gevoren gor freylach,	He was feeling oh so happy,
Iz gevoren gor gor freylach, Elimelech,	Elimelech, he was feeling oh so happy,
Hot er zich gemacht havdole,	So he said the prayer *Havdole,* *
Un geshikt rifn dem shames Naftole,	And he called for Reb Naftole,
Un hot geshikt noch di payklers, di tsvey.	And he called for his drummers to play.
Un az di paykeldike payklers	And when the drummers started drumming,
Hobn paykeldik gepaykelt,	On their drums they were rum-tumming,
Hobn paykeldik gepaykelt, hobn zey.	On their drums they were rum-tumming, right away.
Un az di paykeldike payklers	And when the drummers started drumming,
Hobn paykeldik gepaykelt,	On their drums they were rum-tumming,
Hobn paykeldik gepaykelt, hobn zey.	Cool as cucumbers, those drummers, they did play!

*By this time Rabbi Elimelech is so transported with joy that everything
gets hopelessly mixed up in a wildly repeated last fast section.*

Un az di fideldike tsimblers	And when the fiddlers started drumming
Hobn paykeldik gefidelt,	On their tsimbaloms, so cunning,
Hobn paykeldik gefidelt, hobn zey,	On their drimble-tsimble-fiddlers, right away,
Un az di tsimbeldike payklers	And when the rum-tum-tumming drummers
Hobn fideldik getsimbelt,	Fiddled with the tsimbalomers,
Hobn paykeldik gefidelt, hobn zey.	How those tsimble-fiddle-ummers, they could play!

Havdole — Sabbath prayer

Study for the Torah

Courtesy N.Y. Public Library Picture Collection

Dem Milners Trern
The Miller's Tears

By Mark Warshawsky

This song refers to the expulsion of Jews from their villages, an all-too-common occurence in Tsarist Russia.

Oy, vi fl yo — rn Zay — nen far-fo — rn, Zayt ich bin mil-ner ot o
Could I but num — ber The years that slum — ber, Since I have been a mil-ler

do? Di re — der drey-en zich, Di yo-ren gey-en zich, Ich
here. The wheels keep turn — ing slow, The years, they quick-ly go, And

bin shoyn alt un grayz un gro. Di gro._____
now I'm old and gray, I fear. The fear._____

S'iz teg faranen,
Ch'vil mich dermanen,
Tsi ch'hob gehat a shtikl glik?
    Di reder dreyen zich,
    Di yorn geyen zich, ⎤ 2
Keyn entfer iz nito tsurik. ⎦

Those days are gone by,
And now I ask why:
Did happiness but smile on me?
    The wheels keep turning slow,
    The years, they quickly go. ⎤ 2
No answer ever do I see. ⎦

Ch'hob gehert zogn,
Me vil mich faryogn,
Aroys fun dorf un fun der mil;
    Di reder dreyen zich,
    Di yorn geyen zich, ⎤ 2
Oy, on an ek un on a tsil. ⎦

The order's given,
I will be driven
All from my home and from the mill.
    The wheels keep turning slow,
    The years, they quickly go. ⎤ 2
I have no place to live, and never will. ⎦

Vu vel ich voynen,
Ver vet mich shoynen?
Ich bin shoyn alt, ich bin shoyn mid;
    Di reder dreyen zich,
    Di yorn geyen zich, ⎤ 2
Un oych mit zey geyt oys der yid. ⎦

Where can I go now?
I do not know now,
For I am old and tired, too.
    The wheels keep turning slow,
    The years, they quickly go. ⎤ 2
And with the years will go the Jew. ⎦

Courtesy N.Y. Public Library Picture Collection

Yoshke Fort Avek
Yoshke's Leaving Now

Dating from the Russo-Japanese war of 1905-1905, this moving song was originally intended to ridicule a certain unpleasant Yoshke ("Joey") from Vilna, who had been drafted. Over the years, however, the original intent has been lost and what remains is a tragic wartime dialogue – true for all time.

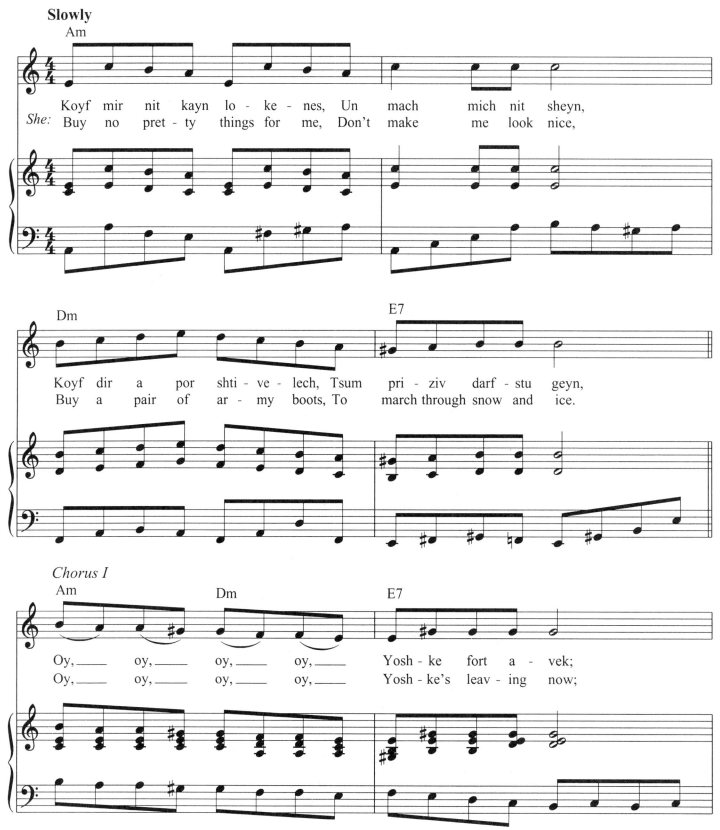

Slowly

She:

Koyf mir nit kayn lo - ke - nes, Un mach mich nit sheyn,
Buy no pret - ty things for me, Don't make me look nice,

Koyf dir a por shti - ve - lech, Tsum pri - ziv darf - stu geyn,
Buy a pair of ar - my boots, To march through snow and ice.

Chorus I

Oy,___ oy,___ oy,___ oy,___ Yosh - ke fort a - vek;
Oy,___ oy,___ oy,___ oy,___ Yosh - ke's leav - ing now;

Noch a sho un noch a sho,___ Der po - yezd geyt a - vek.
In an - oth - er hour or so ___ The train is sure to go.

He: Zay-zhe mir gezunt, Mayn tayere kale. Noch dir vel ich benken Mer vi noch ale.	*He:* Please take good care of yourself My dearest bride, I will long for you, Till once again I'm by your side.

Chorus II   *Chorus II*

Oy, oy, oy, oy,   Oh, oh, oh, oh,
Yoshke fort avek.   Yoshke's leaving now.
Noch a kush un noch a kush,   One more kiss, just one more kiss,
Der poyezd geyt avek.   The train is sure to go.

She: Di ban iz shoyn gekumen Un es chapt mich on a shrek. Lomir zich gezegenen, Der poyezd geyt avek. *Chorus I*	*She:* The train is in the station now, It fills me with fear. We must say goodbye, my darling, Time is growing near. *Chorus I*
He: Klog-zhe nisht un veyn-zhe nisht S'iz altsding blote! Ich vel zayn bay Fonyen* Der shenster in der rote! *Chorus II*	*He:* Do not cry and do not weep, It's not worth a cent. I will be the finest soldier In the regiment. *Chorus II*
She: Droysn iz a zaveruche, Droysn iz a shney, Oy vey, mamele, Dos kepele tut vey! *Chorus II*	*She:* Outside there's a blizzard blowing, And a deep snow. My God, Mother, How my head is filled with woe. *Chorus II*

*"Fonye Ganev" ("Fonye the Thief") was the derisive code name for the tsar among Russian Jews. Conscription into "Fonye's Army" for periods of up to twenty-five years was a real and constant nightmare among Jewish boys aged twelve to eighteen.

Mit A Nodl, On A Nodl
With A Needle, Or Without One

Mit a nodl, on a nodl,
Ney ich mir b'kovod godl.
Mit a nodl, on a nodl,
Ney ich mir b'kovod godl.
  Ich tsi aroys di fastrige,
  Un tu a lek fun mamelige.
Mit a nodl, on a nodl,
Ney ich mir b'kovod godl.

With a needle or without one,
Sewing pleases this devout one.
With a needle or without one,
Sewing pleases this devout one.
  And when I pull out all the basting,
  It's time for *mamelige** tasting.
With a needle or without one,
Sewing pleases this devout one.

Mamelige – A Rumanian cereal or porridge-like delicacy made of cornmeal.

Courtesy N.Y. Public Library Picture Collection

81

Shlof Mayn Kind, Shlof Keseyder
Sleep My Child, Sleep Securely

Az du mayn kind, vest elter vern
Vestu vern mit laytn glaych.
Demolst vestu gevoyre vern
Vost heyst orim uns vos heyst raych.] 2

When you, my child, will grow to manhood,
There is one thing that is sure:
Then you'll see for yourself the great difference –
What is rich and what is poor.] 2

Di tayrste palatsn, di shenste hayzer,
Dos alts macht der oriman.
Nor veystu ver tut in zey voynen?
Gor nisht er, nor der raycher man.] 2

The costly palace, the finest houses,
Are all made by the workingman.
But do you know who lives within these mansions?
Never he – only rich folks can.] 2

Der oriman, er ligt in keler,
Der vilgotsh rint im fun di vent.
Derfun bakumt er a rematn-feler
In di fis un in di hent.] 2

The poor man's home is a dark cellar,
Leaking, dripping, cold as sleet.
And he is bound to get rheumatic fever,
Aches and pains in his hands and feet.] 2

Courtesy N.Y. Public Library Picture Collection

Ot Azoy Neyt A Shnayder
Stitch Away, Little Tailor

Ot a - zoy neyt _ a shnay - der, Ot a - zoy neyt er doch.
Stitch a - way, lit - tle tai - lor, This is how it is done.

Ot a - zoy neyt _ a shnay - der, Ot a - zoy neyt er doch.
Stitch a - way, lit - tle tai - lor, This is how it is done.

Neyt un neyt er a gant - se voch, Far - dint a gil - den mit a loch.
Sews and sews the _ whole week through, And what he earns, it just won't do.

A shnayder neyt un neyt un neyt,
Fardint kadoches, nit kayn broyt.] 2 *Chorus*

A tailor, he does sew and sew,
Instead of bread, he earns just woe.] 2 *Chorus*

Farayorn, nit haynt gedacht,
Hobn mir gehorevet fun acht biz acht.] 2 *Chorus*

A year ago – thank God it's done!
We worked from dawn to setting sun.] 2 *Chorus*

Ober di struktsye hot gemacht,
Mir horeven shoyn mer nit fun acht biz acht.] 2 *Chorus*

But since the union's come our way,
We work no more a twelve-hour day.] 2 *Chorus*

Courtesy N.Y. Public Library Picture Collection

Un Du Akerst
Oh, You Plow

Resolutely

Un du a-kerst, un du zeyst, Un du fi-terst un du meyst;
Oh, you plow and till the land, And you reap with blist-ered hands

Un du ha-merst un du shpinst,___ Zog mein folk___ vos du far-dinst. Kling
And you ham-mer and you spin,___ But what can___ you hope to win?

Klang,___ kling klang,___ Kling der ha-mer mit zayn ge-zang.___ Kling
Oh, the ham-mer sings out its song.___

Klang, Kling Klang, Tse-rayst di key-tn fun sklav-en-tsvang.
It tears the chains that have bound us long.

86

Zog vu iz dayn tish gegreyt,
Zog vu iz dayn yontef-kleyd.
Zog vu iz dayn sharfe shverd
Velechs glik iz dir bashert. *Chorus*

Say, where is your table laid,
And your dress for holiday.
Say, where is your sword of steel,
And what happiness you feel. *Chorus*

Man fun arbet, oyfgevacht!
Un derken dayn shtarke macht.
Ven dayn shtarke hant nor vil,
Shteyen ale reder shtil. *Chorus*

Workers of the world, unite!
You possess unbounded might.
It is up to your free will
If the wheels turn or stand still. *Chorus*

Courtesy N.Y. Public Library Picture Collection

Dire Gelt
Rent Money

The neighborhood of Hester, Norfolk, and Essex Streets presents a quaint scene. The streets are black with purchasers, and bright with the glare of hundreds of torches from the pushcarts. The ... voices of the peddlers crying their wares, the expostulations of the purchasers, the minging of the "Yiddish" of the elders with the English of the young people, make a strange medley of sounds....It is estimated that there are 1,500 peddlers of various wares in that vicinity. The regular peddler pays $25 a year for his license with additional fees to the police. He can hardly earn more than $5 a week so he often hires a pushcart for his wife, and sometimes the children too are brought into the service. The rent of a pushcart is 10 cents a day. Many of the peddlers are only temporarily in the trade. Tailors or mechanics who are out of work hire a pushcart until they find a position. Recently landed immigrants are advised by their friends to take a pushcart until they can establish themselves in some business.

—New York Tribune, September 15, 1898

With a bounce

Di - re gelt,___ un oy, oy, oy,___ Di - re gelt,___ un bo - zhe moy,
Rent is due,___ and oy, oy, oy,___ Rent is due,___ and *bo - zhe moy,**

Di - re gelt,___ un gra - do - voy,___ Di - re gelt muz men tsol - n.
Rent is due,___ and it's no joy,___ Rent is due; time to pay up.

Verse – recitative

Kumt a - rayn der struzh,___ Nemt er a - rop dos hit - l, Un
Now, here comes the land - lord, see how he doffs his hat,___ But

*Bozhe moy – Russian for "My God!"

88

az men tsolt keyn di - re gelt,___ Hengt er a - roys a kvi - tl.
if you don't pay what you owe,___ You're kicked out of your flat.___

Chorus
a tempo

Di - re gelt,___ un oy, oy, oy. Di - re gelt,___ un bo - zhe moy.
Rent is due,___ and oy, oy, oy. Rent is due,___ and *bo - zhe moy.*

Di - re gelt,___ un gra - do - voy,___ Di - re gelt muz men tsol - n.
Rent is due,___ and it's no joy,___ Rent is due; time to pay up.

D. C., then to next verse.
Last time al Fine

Kumt arayn der balabos,	Now here comes the landlord,
Mit dem grobn shtekn,	With his fancy cane.
Un az me git im kayn dire gelt,	And if you don't pay what is due,
Shtelt er aroys di betn. *Chorus & D. C.*	Eviction is his game. *Chorus & D. C.*
Farvos zol ich tsoln dire gelt,	Why do I have to pay rent?
Az di kich iz tsubrochn?	My kitchen is all broken.
Farvos zol ich gebn dire gelt	Why do I have to give him rent,
Az ich hob nisht af vos tsu kochn? *Chorus & D. C.*	Since I cannot do my cooking? *Chorus & D. C.*

Bulbes
Potatoes

Broyt mit bulbes,	Bread with 'taters,
Fleysh mit bulbes,	Meat with 'taters,
Varimes un vetshere – bulbes,	Morning and evening – 'taters.
Ober un vider – bulbes.	Over and over – 'taters.
Ober eynmol in a novine a bulbe kigele!	Ah, the treat we love to eat – potato pudding!
Un zuntik vayter bulbes.	And Sunday, once more, 'taters.
Ober – bulbes,	Once more – 'taters,
Vider – bulbes,	Later – 'taters,
Ober un vider – bulbes,	Once more and later – 'taters.
Vider un ober – bulbes!	Later and once more, – 'taters,
Ober shabes nochn tsholnt a bulbe kigele!	Ah, but Sabbath with the roast we have potato pudding!
Un zuntik vayter, bulbers.	And Sunday, once more, 'taters.

Courtesy N.Y. Public Library Picture Collection

Elis Ayland
Ellis Island

All passenger vessels are boarded at Quarantine by inspectors from the Immigration Bureau...and if any passenger is thought to be a person who comes within the restrictive clauses of the law he is compelled to go to Ellis Island and await investigation....As an instance of the care that is exercised to prevent improper persons from landing, statistics show that as many as 800 immigrants have been detained and returned to their homes in Italy in one month. *(The New York Times, January 31, 1897)*

O El - is Ay - land, Du gre - nets fun fray - land, Vi
O El - lis Is - land, You bor - der of free - land, How

groys un vi shrek - lech du bist! A - zel - che r'-
big and how fear - ful you are! You vis - it such

tsi - ches Dos ke - nen nor ru - ches. Du plagst di ge - plag - te um -
crimes with - out rea - son or rhyme on the peo - ple who come from a -

A Briv Fun Amerike
A Letter From America

I am a greenhorn, being only five months out of Odessa, and I cannot forgive myself for being in America now. My head and heart ache when I read in your paper that thousands of workers stand on the barricades in Russia and fight like lions...Oh, how I would like to be there in the midst of battle, to stand shoulder to shoulder with my comrades that my blood, too, may make our flag red. But the great ocean does not permit one to flee without a ticket, and the boat and railroad do not want to know of my thoughts, and they say that without the dollars they will not take me. Money to pay I have not. What shall I do? (From a letter to the editor of the *Jewish Forward* by Joseph Thest, January 20, 1906)

Slowly

Tay - e - re ma - me, tay - e - re mut - ter,
Dear - est ma - ma, dear - est moth - er,

Du ____ mayn tay - er ko ____ sher ____ harts, Tsu
My ____ dear heart, let me ____ ex - plain. Do

veys - tu vi ich veyn a - zoy bi - ter, Un ____ vi ____ tif iz
you ____ know why I cry ____ so bit - ter, And ____ the ____ depth of

Eyn Zach Vel Ich
Only One Thing I Ask

When Tsar Alexander II was assassinated by revolutionary terrorists on March 1, 1881, the modest attempts at liberalism *vis-à-vis* the Russian Jews came to an abrupt end. With the accession of Alexander III came a wave of bloody pogroms and persecutions that set into motion a monumental exodus.

The first Jewish immigrants had arrived in the Dutch colony of New Amsterdam as early as 1654. Over the intervening two centuries, a slow trickle of Jews (some 7,500 between 1820 and 1850, for example) had made their way to the New World. By the 1870s that trickle had grown substantially, as over 40,000 new arrivals were counted. Emigration up to that point was, however, a decision prompted by individual desire. The reign of terror of Alexander III changed all that. Now it became literally a question of collective survival.

From the text of this song we know that the singer is a Russian Jew, with an imperfect awareness of American society (believing that slavery still existed), but so desperate to leave Russia that he would even sell himself into bondage.

Moderately

Eyn zach vel ich Got bay dir be-tn, az di zach __ zol mir zayn __ ba - shert; Fun Rus-land muz ich op-tre - tn, Keyn A - me-ri - ke vet zayn __ mayn pa - chod. Fun

On-ly one thing I ask of you __ God, and I hope __ it __ be __ my __ fate; From Rus-sia I must de-part __ now, To A - me-ri - ca I now __ turn my gait. I

key - ne gli - kn veys ich___ nit, in Rus - land is mir zey- er shlect.
know no hap - pi - ness at___ all, in Rus - sia things are ver - y grave.

Keyn A - me - ri - ke muz ich op - fo - rn, far - koy - fn vel ich zich far a knecht.
For A - me - ri - ca I have to leave now, to sell my- self as a low- ly slave.

Kolumbus, Ich Hob Tsu Dir Gornit
Columbus, I Give You The First Prize

Christopher Columbus was held personally responsible for all the good and bad that was encountered in America. When things went well, he got the "first prize". When things didn't quite work out his name became a malediction.

Ko - lum - bus, ich hob tsu dir gor - nit._____ Tsu
Co - lum - bus, I give you the first prize. _____ To

dir, mayn A - me - ritsh-ke, shur nit._____ Siz mir voyl, es
you, my A - me - ri - ca, like-wise._____ All is fine as

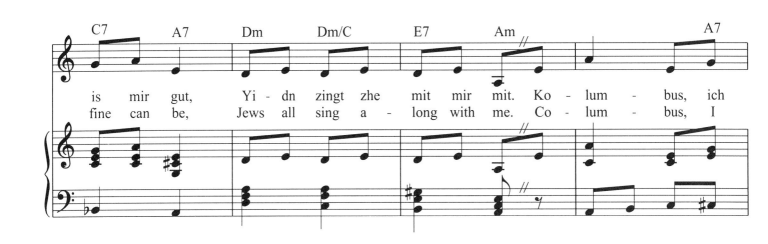

is mir gut, Yi - dn zingt zhe mit mir mit. Ko - lum - bus, ich
fine can be, Jews all sing a - long with me. Co - lum - bus, I

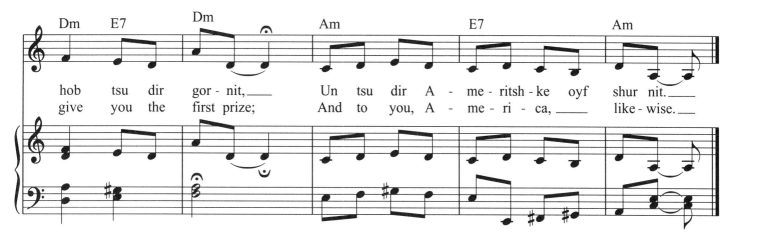

hob tsu dir gor - nit,____ Un tsu dir A - me - ritsh - ke oyf shur nit.____
give you the first prize; And to you, A - me - ri - ca, ____ like - wise. ____

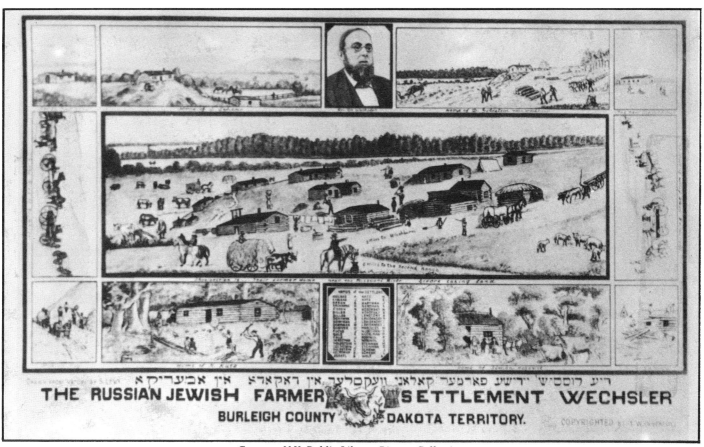

Courtesy N.Y. Public Library Picture Collection

Di Grine Kuzine
The Greenhorn Cousin

This is arguably the most famous of all Jewish immigration songs. My mother sang it to the rhythm of the sewing machines along with other young Jewish and Italian working women in New York's garment district. It was often sung lightly or hummed without paying too much attention to the words, which recount one of the recurring tragedies of immigrant life. Here again we find Columbus involved in the fate of the new arrival.

Words by Hyman Prizant
Music by Abe Schwartz

Es iz tsu mir ge-ku-men a ku-zi - ne.
A cous-in came to me, just like a new - born.

Sheyn vi gold iz zi ge-ven, di gri - ne. Di
Good as gold she was, this pret-ty green - horn, Her

be-ke-lekh vi roy-te po-me-ran - tsn,
ros-y cheeks we all found so en-tranc - ing,

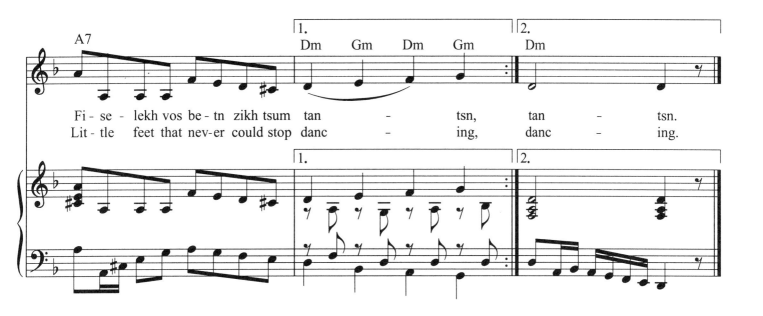

Fi - se - lekh vos be - tn zikh tsum tan - tsn, tan - tsn.
Lit - tle feet that nev - er could stop danc - ing, danc - ing.

Nit gegangen iz zi – nor geshprungen,
Nit geredt hot zi, nor gezungen;
Freylekh, lustik iz geven ir mine.
Ot aza geven iz mayn kuzine.] 2

Ikh bin arayn tsu mayn "nekst-dorke"
Vos zi hot a "milineri-storke,"
A "dzhab" gekrogn hob ikh far mayn kuzine –]
Az lebn zol di goldene medine!] 2

Avek zaynen fun demolt on shoyn yorn,
Fun mayn kuzine iz a tel gevorn;
"Peydes" yorn lang hot zi geklibn,]
Biz fun ir aleyn iz nisht geblibn.] 2

Unter ire bloye sheyne oygn
Shvartse pasn hobn zikh fartsoygn;
Di bekelekh, di royte pomerantsn,]
Hobn zikh shoyn oysgegrint in gantsn.] 2

Haynt, as ikh bagegn mayn kuzine
Un ikh freg zi: Vos zhe makhstu, grine?
Entfert zi mir mit a krumer mine:]
– Az brenen zol Kolombuses medine!] 2

Never walking – always lightly springing,
Never talking – always brightly singing,
Full of joy – and smiles a dime a dozen;]
That's the way she carried on, my cousin.] 2

I dropped in to visit my "next-doorkeh,"[1]
The one who has a millinery "storkeh."[2]
For my cousin I found some employment,]
And that was the end of her enjoyment.] 2

Since that fateful day my cousin blew in,
The poor girl has just become a ruin;
Years of paydays – working, slaving, straining,]
'Til of her there was nothing more remaining.] 2

Underneath her once blue, pretty eyes now
Dark black lines of sorrow do arise now,
And her rosy cheeks, so full of color –]
All you see now is a sickly pallor.] 2

Nowadays, if I should meet my cousin,
And I ask her, "Greeny, so what's buzzin'?"
Bitterly she answers, "Understand now –]
Devil take Columbus's new land now!"] 2

1. Yiddish-English for "female next-door neighbor."
2. Yiddish-English diminutive for "store."

Eyder Ich Leyg Mich Shlofn
No Sooner Do I Lie Down

Moderately

Ey - der ich leyg mich shlo - fn, Darf ich shoyn oyf - shteyn, Mit
No soon-er do I lie down, Then I must get up. I

may - ne kran - ke bey - ner Tsu der ar - beit geyn.
drag my ach - ing bod - y To the cruel sweat - shop.

Chorus

Tsu got vel ich vey - nen, ___ Mit a groys ge - veyn.
To God will I cry, Oh, ___ Lord, please an - swer me.

Vos ich bin ge - boy - rn A ne - to - rn tsu zayn.
Was I real - ly born, Just a poor seam-stress to be?

Ch'kum shpet tsu der arbet
S'iz doch vayt der veg,
Shlogt men mir op
Far halbe teg.   *Chorus*

Di nodlen vern tsubrochn
Fuftsn a menut.
Di finger vern tsushtochn,
Es rint fun zey dos blut.   *Chorus*

Ich layd shtendig hunger
Ich hob nit vos tsu esn.
Vil ich gelt betn,
Heyst men mir fargesn.   *Chorus*

If I'm late to work,
Since I live far away,
Then I am docked,
Docked a half-day's pay.   *Chorus*

The needles, they get broken,
Fifteen at a time.
Our fingers, they are bleeding –
It's a dirty crime.   *Chorus*

I am always hungry,
With not enough to eat.
If I ask for more money –
I'm out on the street.   *Chorus*

Courtesy N.Y. Public Library Picture Collection

Mayn Rue Plats
My Resting Place

Morris Rosenfeld (1862-1923) has the distinction of being the first Yiddish poet to have had his works translated into English (in 1898, by Leo Weiner, a professor of Slavic languages at Harvard University: *Songs from the Ghetto).* His fame spread back across the Atlantic, where his works were also translated into French, German, Polish, Bohemian, and Russian (the Russian edition was brought out by Maxim Gorki). He even made a European tour, reading his poems in Yiddish to enthusiastic audiences. His poems are all the more stirring because they were written from his actual experiences bent over machines in sweatshops and as a union delegate.

By Morris Rosenfeld

Calmly

Nit zuch mich vu di mir - tn grin - en, Ge - finst mich
Don't look for me where myr - tles blos - som, Dear, there you'll

dor - tn nit, mayn shats. Vu le - bens vel - kn bay ma -
nev - er see my face. Where lives are wast - ed in the

shi - nen; Dor - tn iz mayn ru - e plats. Dor - tn
fac - t'ry; There you'll find my rest - ing place, There you'll

iz _____ mayn ru - e plats.
find _____ my rest - ing place.

Nit zuch mich vu di feygl zingen.
Gefinst mich dortn nit, mayn shats.
A shklaf bin ich, vu keytn klingen;
Dortn iz mayn rue plats,
Dortn iz mayn rue plats.

Don't look for me where birds are singing,
Dear, there you'll never see my face.
A slave am I where chains are ringing;
There you'll find my resting place,
There you'll find my resting place.

Nit zuch mich vu fontanen shpritsn.
Gefinst mich dortn nit, mayn shats.
Vu trern rinen, tseyner kritsn;
Dortn iz mayn rue plats,
Dortn iz mayn rue plats.

Don't look for me 'mong fountains splashing,
Dear, there you'll never see my face.
Where tears are flowing, teeth are gnashing;
There you'll find my resting place,
There you'll find my resting place.

Un libstu mich mit varer libe,
To kum tsu mir mayn guter shats,
Un hayter oyf mayn harts dos tribe,
Un mach mir zis mayn rue plats,
Un mach mir zis mayn rue plats.

And if your love is truly burning,
Then come to me in fond embrace,
And put an end to all my yearning,
And make it sweet – my resting place,
And make it sweet – my resting place.

Courtesy N.Y. Public Library Picture Collection

In Kamf
In Struggle

In the decade between 1880 and 1890, 5,246,613 immigrants entered the United States. Among them, in 1881, was David Edelstadt, who came to America at the age of fifteen after escaping the terrible Kiev pogrom of May 8, 1881. He found employment in sweatshops and subsequently contracted tuberculosis. Because of his personal tragedy he was able to express in his poetry the sentiments of the exploited immigrant worker. He died in 1892 at the age of twenty-six.

In 1876 the Russian poet G. A. Machtet (1852-1901) wrote a poem entitled "Tortured to Death in Captivity," dedicated to martyred student revolutionaries of the 1870s. It was set to a melody of unknown origin and became a traditional song of mourning among Russian revolutionaries. David Edelstadt, who wrote *In Kamf* in 1889, certainly knew the Russian song, and found that his poem was admirably complemented by that melody. *In Kamf* was soon elevated to the status of a quasi-official hymn of Jewish workers all over the world. It enjoyed such popularity and was sung with such fervor at workers' meetings and demonstrations, that Morris Rosenfeld called it the Jewish "Marseillaise."

By David Edelstadt

Mir vern dershosn, gehangen,
Men roybt undz dos lebn un recht;
Derfar vayl mir emes farlangen
Un frayhayt far oreme knecht,
Un frayhayt far oreme knecht.

By gun and by rope and by fire
They steal our rights and our lives;
Because of our one true desire:
Freedom for poor working slaves,
Freedom for poor working slaves.

Shmidt undz in ayzerne keytn,
Vi blutike chayes undz rayst;
Ir kent undzer kerper nor teytn
Nor keyn mol undzer heylikn gayst.
Nor keyn mol undzer heylikn gayst.

Cast us in cold iron shackles,
Like beasts to destroy us you try.
It's only our bodies you're killing,
But our spirit never will die,
But our spirit never will die.

Ir kent undz dermordn, tiranen,
Naye kemfer vet brengen di tsayt;
Un mir kemfn, mir kemfn biz vanen
Di gantse velt vet vern bafrayt,
Di gantse velt vet vern bafrayt.

You tyrants can try to destroy us;
New soldiers will answer the call.
To battle, to battle till that day
When we have brought freedom to all,
When we have brought freedom to all.

To Gey Zich Lernen Tantsn
Just Go And Learn To Dance Now

An American Jewish song of the 1970s, reflecting still another migration.

Lively

"A gut mor - gn, dir, Reb Ber - l." "A gut mor - gn Sa - mi." "Ich
"A good morn - ing, friend, Reb Ber - l." "A good morn - ing Sam - my." "They

hob ge - hert az geyst, mit ma - zl, bley - ben in Mi - a - mi.
tell me that you are now going to stay here in Mi - a - mi.

Trogst oyf, sich koym zi - bn tsen - dlik yo - re - lach in gan - tsn;
Though you're push - ing sev - en - ty, you have - n't lost the chance now,

Heybst du on a tsvey - te yu - gend, To gey zich ler - nen tan - tsn."
To be - gin a sec - ond child - hood, Just go and learn to dance now."

Chorus

Tra la la la la. la la la, La la la, la la la,

Tra la la la la la la, La la la, la la la la.

Vakst sich shmaltsik di osobe,	Putting on a little weight now.
Es vakst on kvelt di talye,	And your waist is spreading,
On dos kleyne klapmashindl	And your ticker's working harder–
Iz sheyn etvas kalye.	Who knows where you're heading!
Nor der chayshik iz faran,	But you are as strong as ever,
On di oygen glantsn.	Bright, your eyes are glancing.
Heybst du an a tsveyten yugend,	To begin a second childhood,
To gey zich lernen tantsn. *Chorus*	Go and take up dancing. *Chorus*
Plonterst zich in karohodl?	Struggle through a circle dance,
Trachst nit fun keyn yorn.	Awkward though you may be,
Heybst du on a tsveyte yugend,	You'll begin a second childhood,
Glaych vi naygeborn.	Like a newborn baby.
Az du bist shoyn a ben shabim,	Three-score-ten you'll soon be turning,
Dos farges in gantsn.	Life is still entrancing.
Heybst du an a tsveyte yugend,	To begin a second childhood,
To gey zich lernen tantsn. *Chorus*	Go and take up dancing. *Chorus*

Unter Di Churves Fun Poyln
Under The Ruins Of Poland

Slowly

Un - ter di chur - ves fun Poy - ln, A kop mit blon - de
Un - der the ru - ins of Po - land, There lies a small blond

hor,_____ Der kop un say___ der chur - bn,_____
head. The blond head and ___ the ru - ins,_____

Bey - de ze - nen vor._____ Dol - ye, may - ne dol - ye._____
Both of them ___ are dead._____ Sor - row, oh, my sor - row._____

Chorus

Dol - ye, dol - ye may - ne._____ may - ne._____
Sor - row, oh, - my sor - row._____ sor - row._____

Iber di churves fun polyn
Falt un falt der shney,
Der blonder kop fun mayn meydl
Tut mir mesukn vey.   *Chorus*

Der veytik zitst baym shraybtish
Un shraybt a langn briv,
Di trer in zayne oygn,
Iz emesdik un tif.   *Chorus*

Iber di churves fun poyln
Flatert a foygl um
A groyser shive-foygl,
Er tsitert mit di fligl frum.   *Chorus*

Der groyser shive-foygl
(Mayn dershlogn gemit),
Er trogt oyf zayne fligl
Dos dozike troyer-lid.   *Chorus*

Over the ruins of Poland
Falls and falls the snow.
The blond head of my daughter
Brings me terrible woe.   *Chorus*

The pain sits at my table,
And writes an endless tale.
The tears that it is shedding,
They are profound and real.   *Chorus*

Over the ruins of Poland
A fluttering bird is there.
The bird is deep in mourning,
It trembles in the air.   *Chorus*

And that great bird of mourning
(O, my soul, how long!),
Upon its wings it carries
This very mourning song.   *Chorus*

111

Aroys Iz In Vilne A Nayer Bafel
In Vilna Was Issued A Brand-New Decree

In April 1943 the Gestapo rounded up the last four thousand Jews of the province of Vilna, Lithuania, from the towns of Oshmene, Soler, Tal, Sventsian, Vidz, and others and brought them to the city of Vilna. From there they were supposed to be transferred to the Kovno ghetto, but this was only a pretext — the closed cattle cars in which the people were being transported went only as far as the nearby town of Ponar. At that point the slaughter began and the Jews realized their deception too late. Nevertheless, many of them desperately attacked their guards with fists, clubs, and even teeth. Several Germans were killed in the melee. About thirty Jews escaped.

Moderately

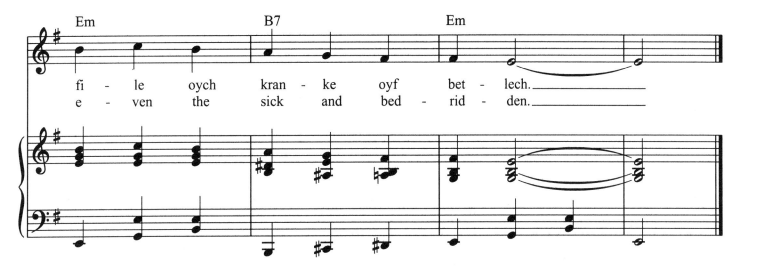

fi - le oych kran - ke oyf bet - lech._____
e - ven the sick and bed - rid - den._____

Tsunoyfgeshpart hot men dem lager,	The camp became crowded with thousands of Jews,
Men hot zey genumen sortirn:	And then they began the selection:
Oshmene Yidn in Vilne tsu blaybn,	Jews from Oshemene in Vilna would stay,
Un Soler in Kovne tsu firn.	Send Solers in Kovno's direction.
Aroysgefirt hot men fun lager,	The first group of martyrs was led from the camp.
Yunge un frishe korbones,	"More victims!" the order was worded.
Arayngeshpart hot men zey alemen glaych	Then jammed all together like animals,
In di zelbe farmachte vagones.	They into the sealed boxcars were herded.
Der tsug iz sich langsam geforn,	Then slowly the train made its way down the tracks,
Gefayft un gegebn sirenes.	The whistles and sirens were blowing.
Stantsie Ponar – der tsug shtelt zich op,	But when it reached Ponar it came to a halt,
Men tshepet dort op di vagones.	And then the uncoupling got going.
Zey hobn derzen az men hot zey farfirt,	They realized then that they had been betrayed,
Men firt tsu der shreklicher sh'chite.	And that they would be killed at the station.
Zey hobn tsebrochn di tir fun vagon,	So, smashing the door to the box car,
Genumen aleyn machn pleyte.	They all tried escaping in great desperation.
Zey hobn gevorfn zich af der geshtapo,	They threw themselves bodily on the Gestapo,
Un zey di kleyder tserisn.	Biting and clawing and crying;
Geblibn zaynen lign lebn di yidn,	And next to the bodies of Jews on the ground,
Etleche Daytshn tsebisn.	Several Germans were lying.
S'hobn di getos fun der provints,	From ghettos of all of the province around,
Gegebn fir toyznt korbones.	Some four thousand martyrs were given,
Un opgefirt hot men di zachn fun zey,	And all their belongings were shipped back again
Tsurik in di zelbe vagones,	In the same cars in which they'd been driven.

Shtil, Di Nacht
Still, The Night

This is a Jewish partisan song dating from the uprising of the Vilna ghetto against the Nazi army in 1943. See the next song, "Zog Nit Keynmol", for more background on its composer and the circumstances surrounding its composition.

Words and Music by Hirsh Glik

Shtil,   di nacht iz oys - ge - shte - nt,   Un   der frost hot shtark ge -
Still,   the night, and decked with   star - light,   And   the frost burned like fine

brennt.   Tsi ge - denk - stu vi ich hob dich ge - le - rnt
sand.   You re - mem - ber the time that I did teach _____ you

Hal - tn a shpay - er in di hent?   Tsi ge - hent?
To   hold a pis - tol in your hand?   your - hand?

A moyd, a peltsl un a beret,
Un halt in hant fest a nagan.
A moyd nit a sametenem ponim,
Hit op dem soyne's karavan.

Getsilt, geshosn un getrofn!
Hot ir kleyninker pistoyl.
A oto, a fulinkn mit vofn
Farhaltn hot zi mit eyn koyl!

Fartog, fun vald aroysgekrochn,
Mit shney girlandn oyf di hor.
Gemutikt fun kleyninkn nitsochn
Far undzer nayem, frayen dor!

A girl in furs hides in the forest,
Holding tight a hand grenade.
A girl with a face of smoothest velvet
Strikes at the German's cavalcade.

She aims, she fires true and steady
With her pistol smoking hot.
A transport, loaded down with weapons,
Has been halted with one shot.

At dawn she steals from out the forest,
Snowflakes garlanding her hair.
How proud of her one small winning battle,
Leading to freedom everywhere.

A group of Jewish partisans from Vilna, Lithuania, 1945.
Courtesy N.Y. Public Library Picture Collection

Zog Nit Keynmol
Never Say

In April 1943, the Nazis intensified their round-up of Jews around Vilna, Poland. The Vilna-born poet Hirsh Glik escaped and joined the partisans. It was the time of the heroic uprising of the Warsaw Ghetto, and Glik was inspired to write this song. It soon became the official hymn of the Jewish partisans. With the liquidation of the Vilna Ghetto, Glik was captured by the Gestapo and sent to a concentration camp in Estonia. When the Red Army swept through the area the following year, he escaped from the camp, only to be killed fighting the Germans in the nearby woods. He was twenty-four.

Words and Music by Hirsh Glik

Zog nit keyn-mol az du geyst dem lets-tn veg. Chotsh him-len
Nev - er say that you are on your fi - nal road, Though o - ver-

blay - e - ne far-shte - ln bloy - e teg; Vayl ku - men
head dark skies of lead may death for - bode; The long a-

vet noch und - zer oys - ge-benkt - te sho, Es vet a
wait - ed ho - ur sure - ly's draw - ing near, When with a

Yiddish	English
Fun grinem palmen-land biz vayn land fun shney,	From land of palm tree to the far-off land of snow,
Mir kumen on mit undzer payn, mit undzer vey,	Our people come together crushed by pain and woe.
Un vu gefaln s'iz a shprits fun undzer blut,	But where a drop of our blood has touched the ground,
Shprotsn vet dort undzer gvure undzer mut. $]$ 2	There our strength and our courage will resound. $]$ 2
Dos lid geshriben iz mit blut un nit mit blay,	This song is written down with blood and not with lead,
S'iz nit a lidl fun a foygl oyf der fray.	The birds don't sing it, for it fills the air with dread.
Dos hot a folk ts'vishn falndike vent	This song was sung as all around us bullets sprayed,
Dos lid gezungen mit naganes in di hent! $]$ 2	And walls collapsed as people hurled their hand grenades. $]$ 2

Courtesy N.Y. Public Library Picture Collection